Tiki Ty's
Pin-UP girl
COLORING BOOK
#3

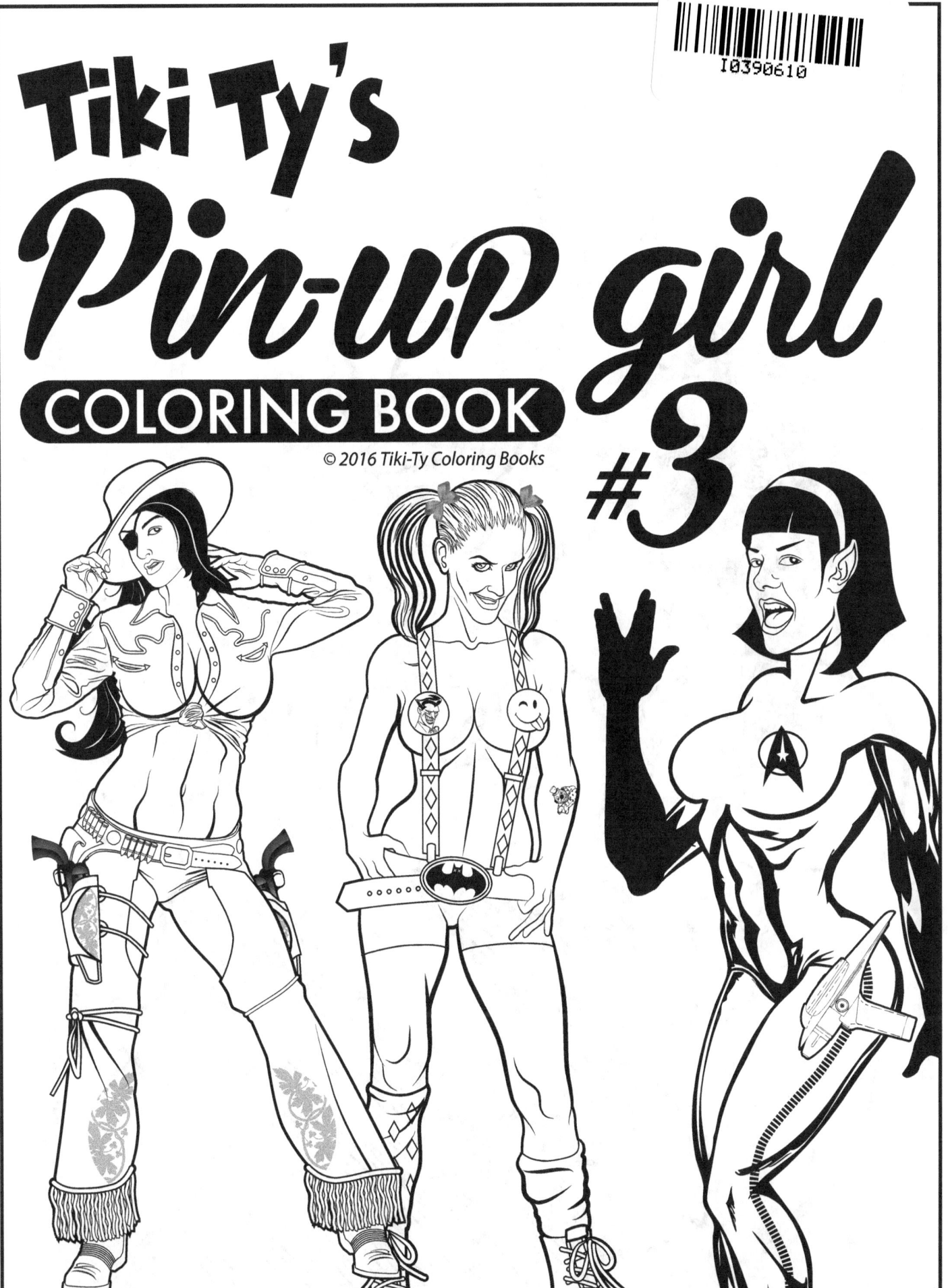

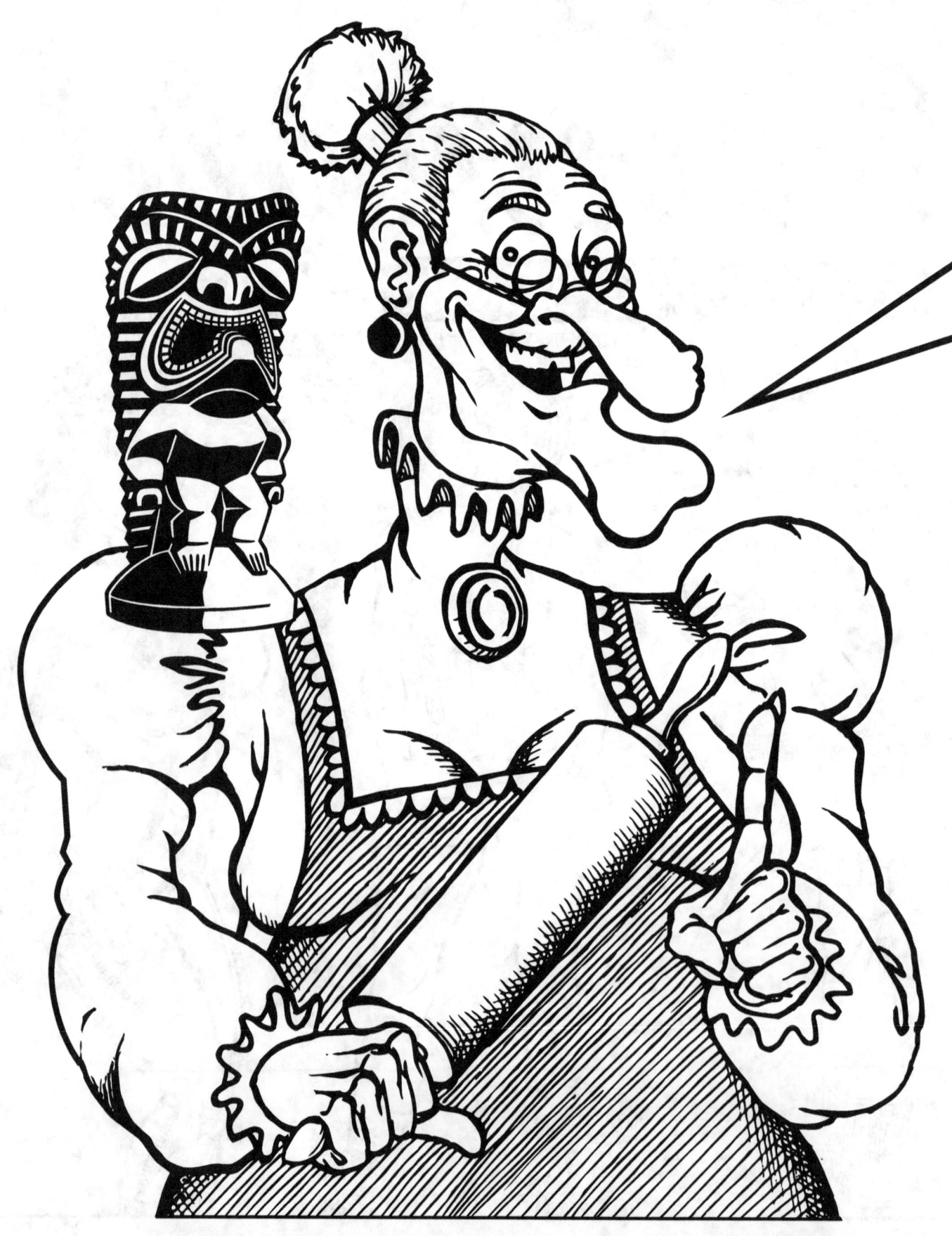

YES DEAR READER YOUR PRAYERS & XMAS LETTERS HAVE BEEN ANSWERED. YOU HOLD IN YOUR HANDS ANOTHER ISSUE OF TIKI-TY COLORING FUN. AND THIS ONE IS #3 OF MY PINUP ART SERIES, I HOPE YOU ENJOY!

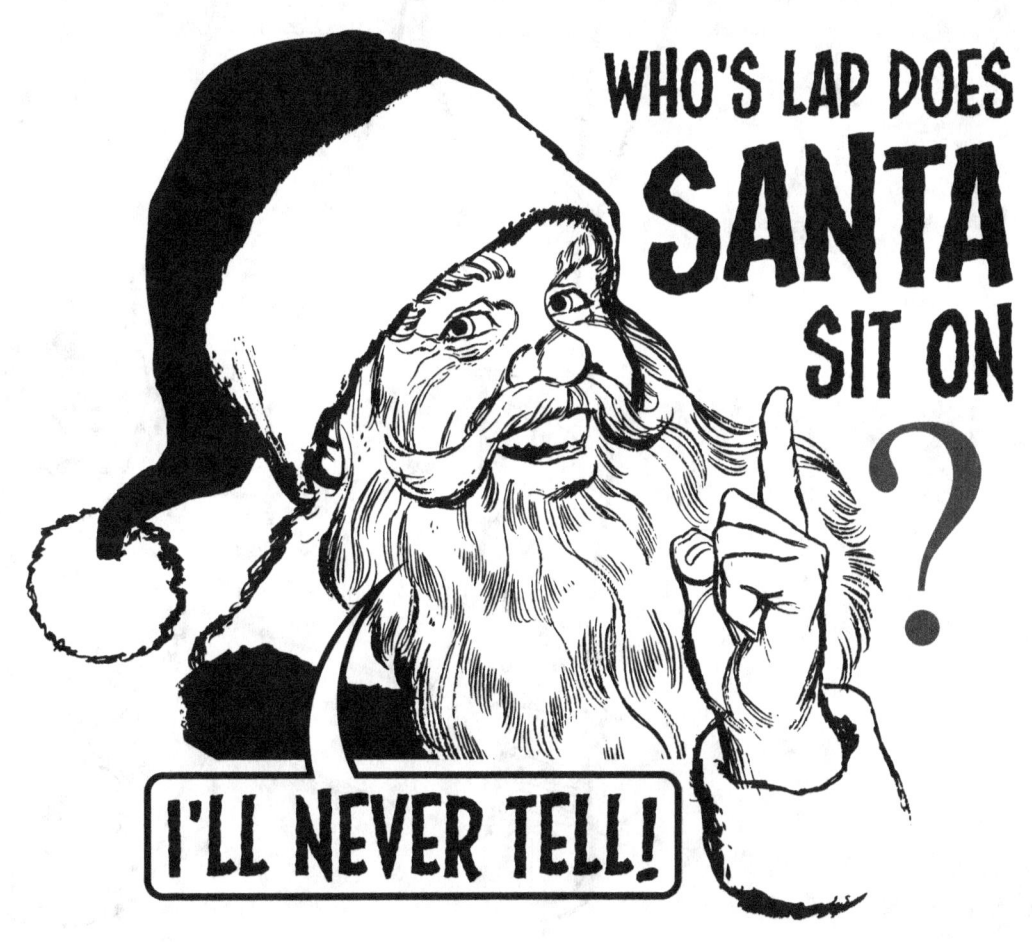

WHO'S LAP DOES SANTA SIT ON ?

I'LL NEVER TELL!

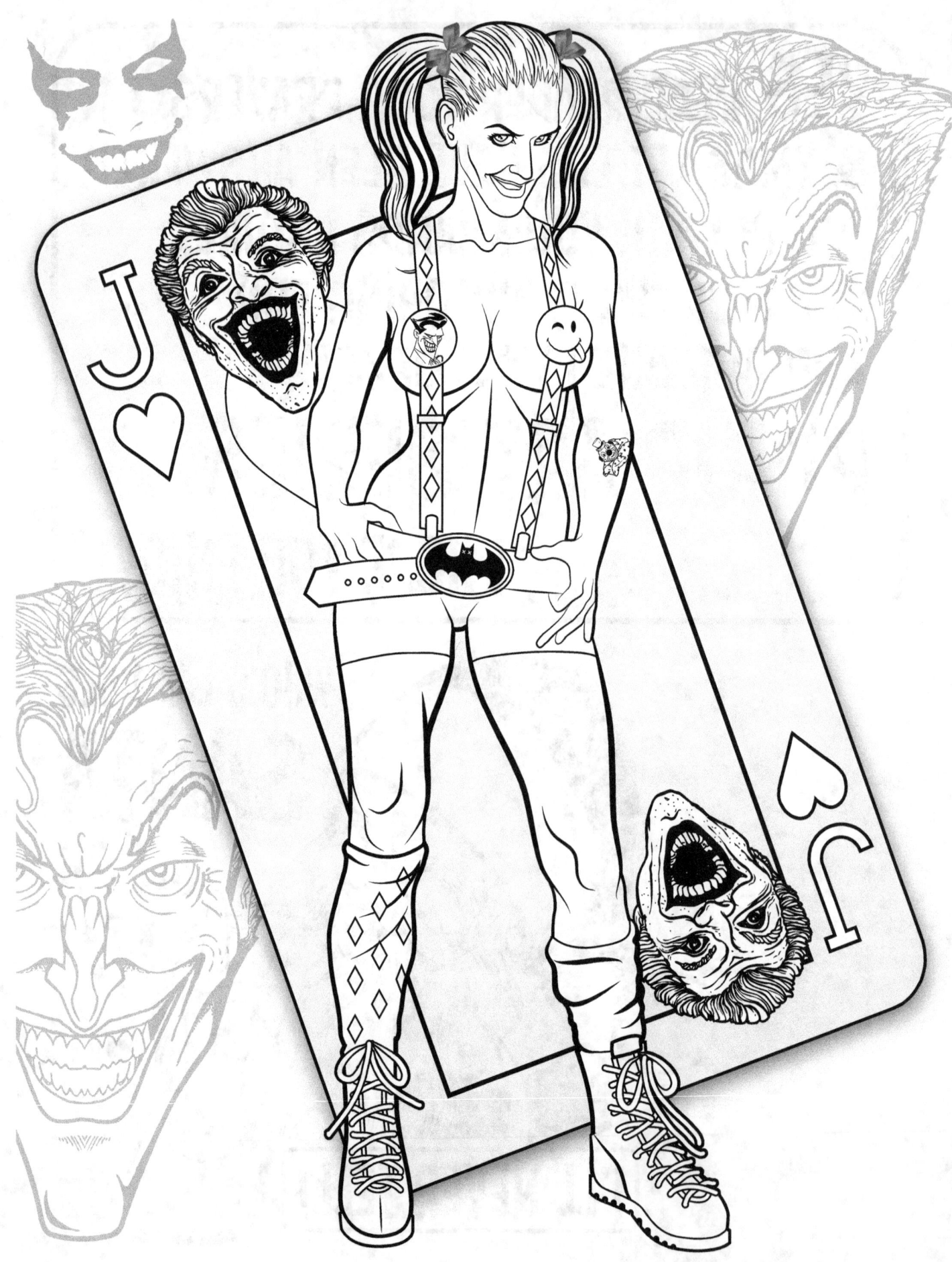

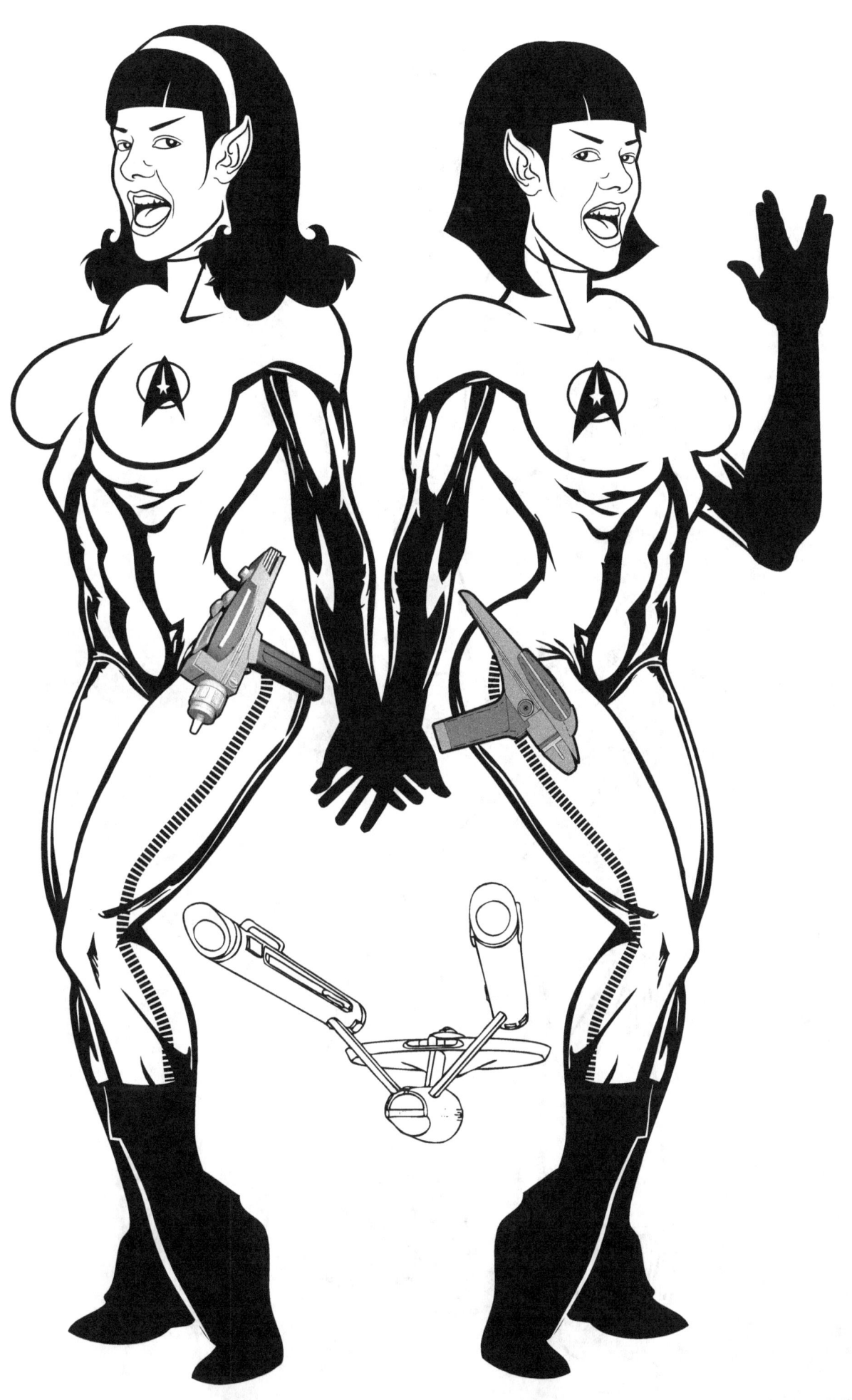

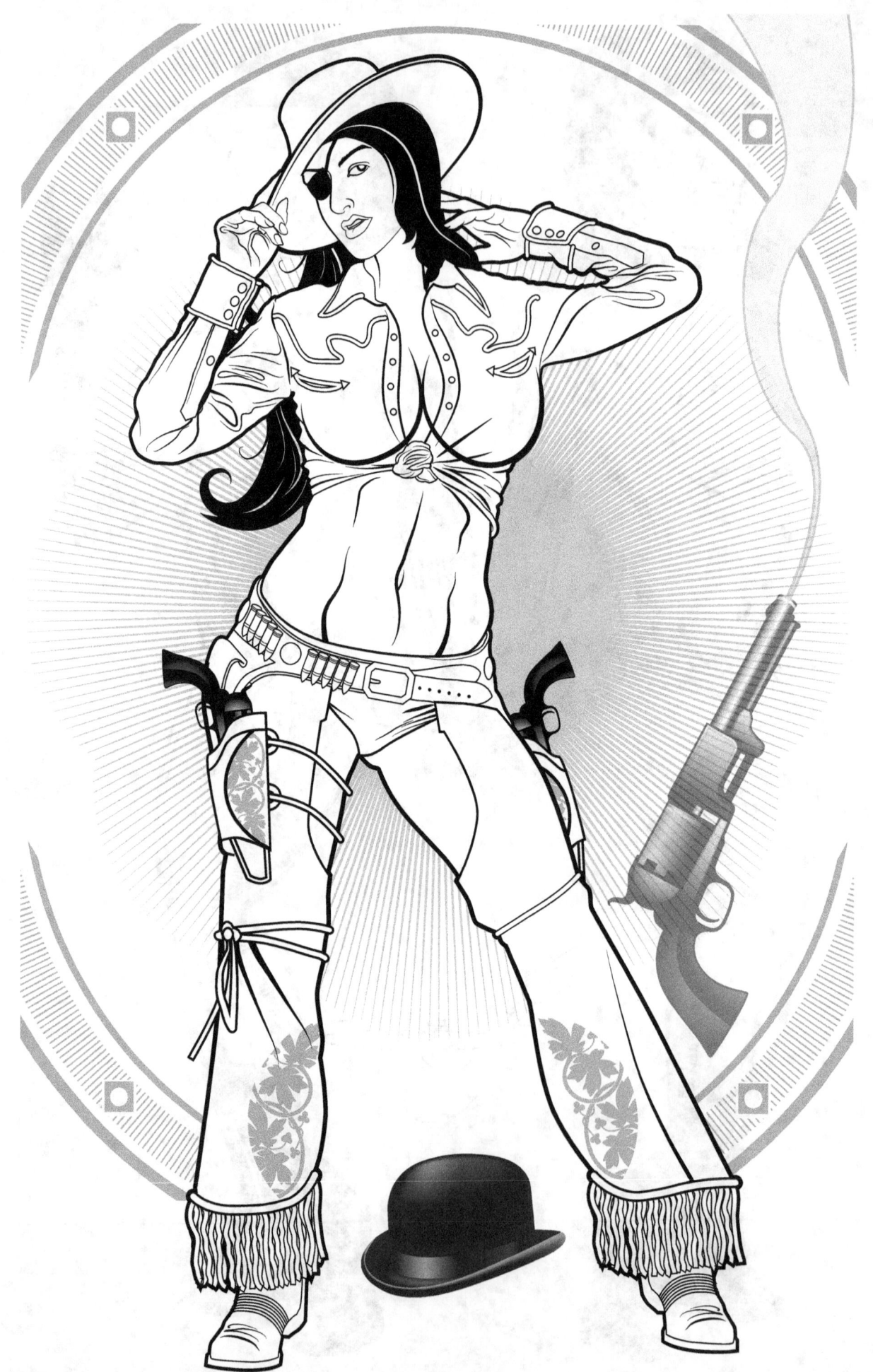

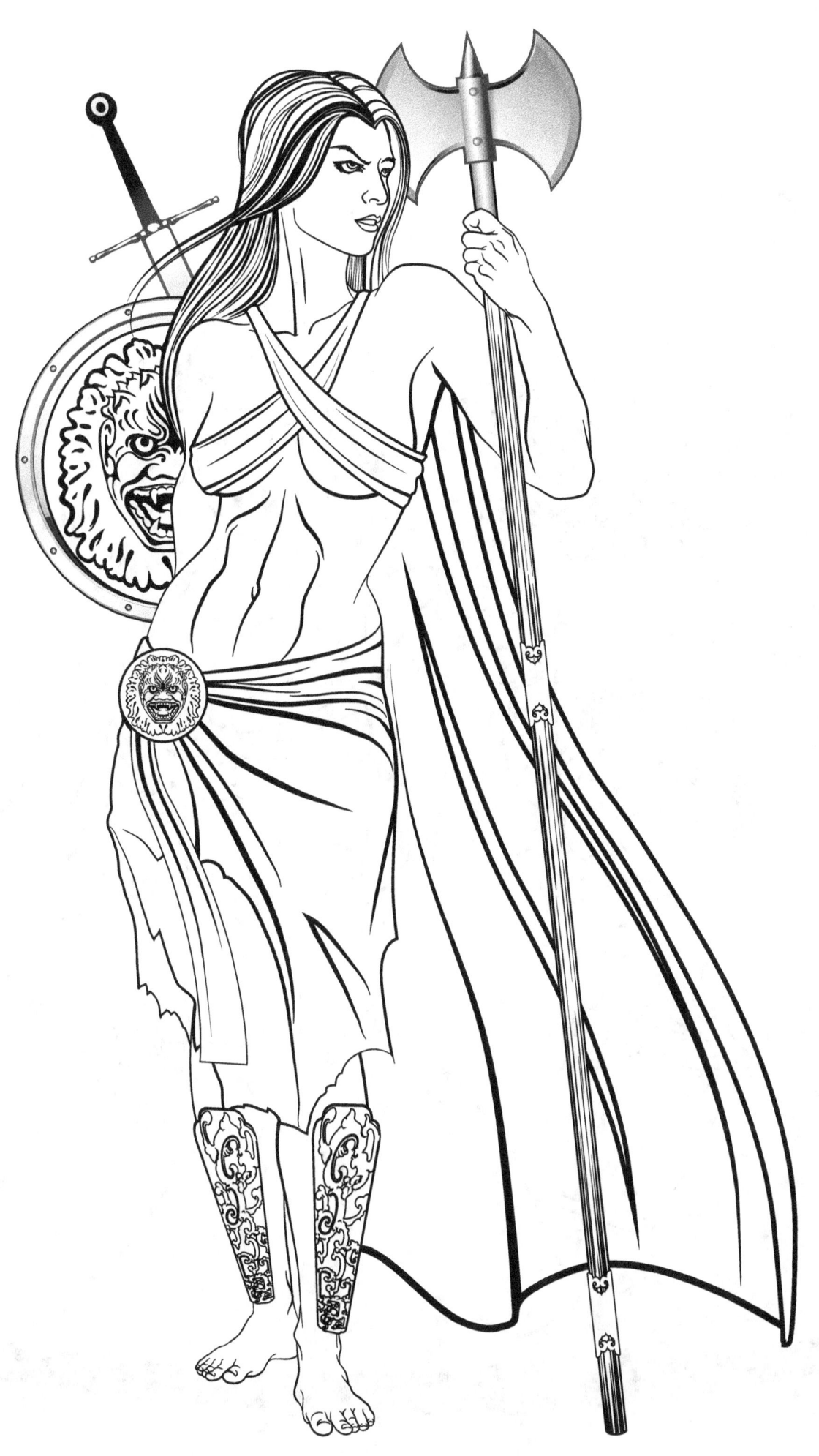

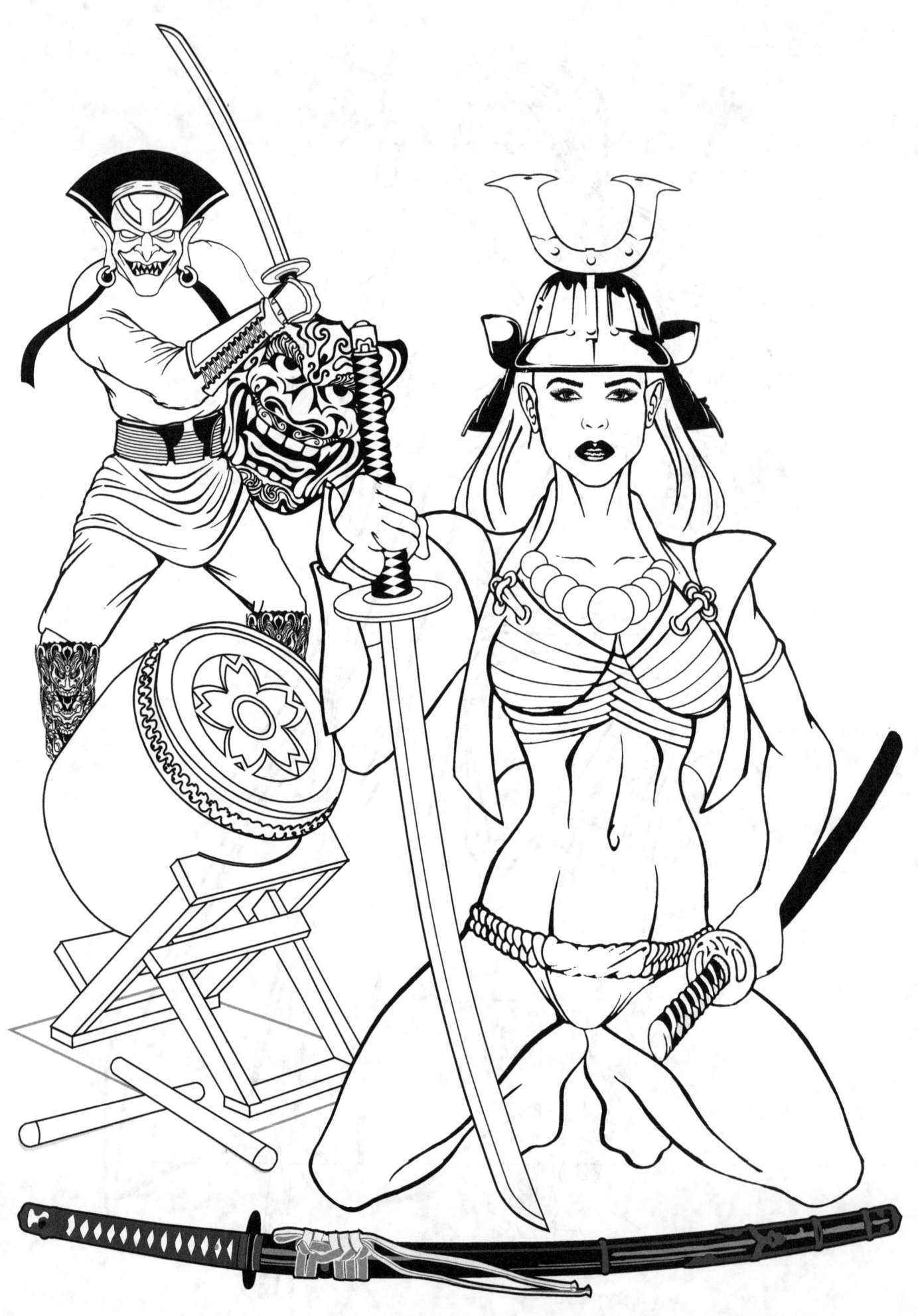

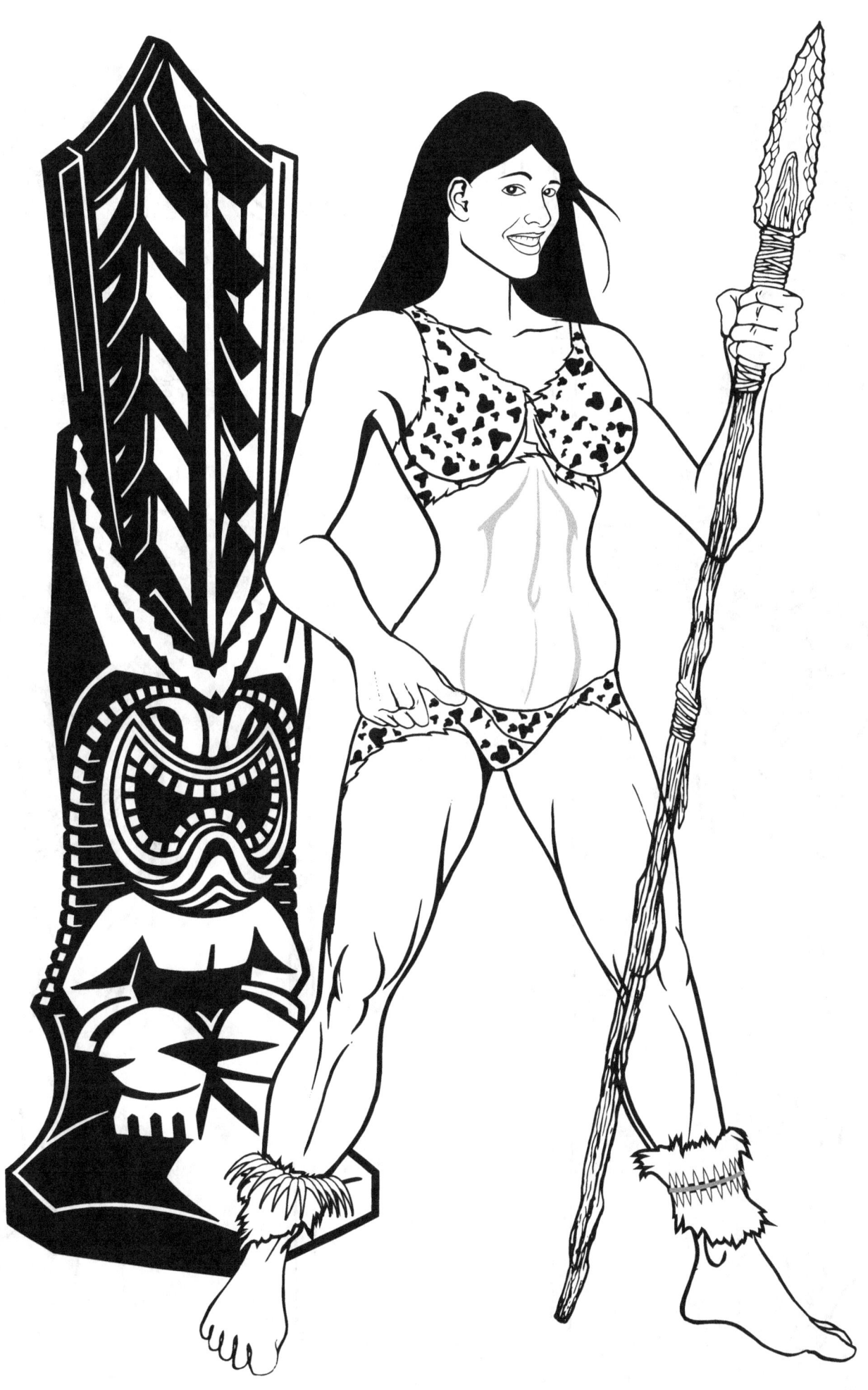

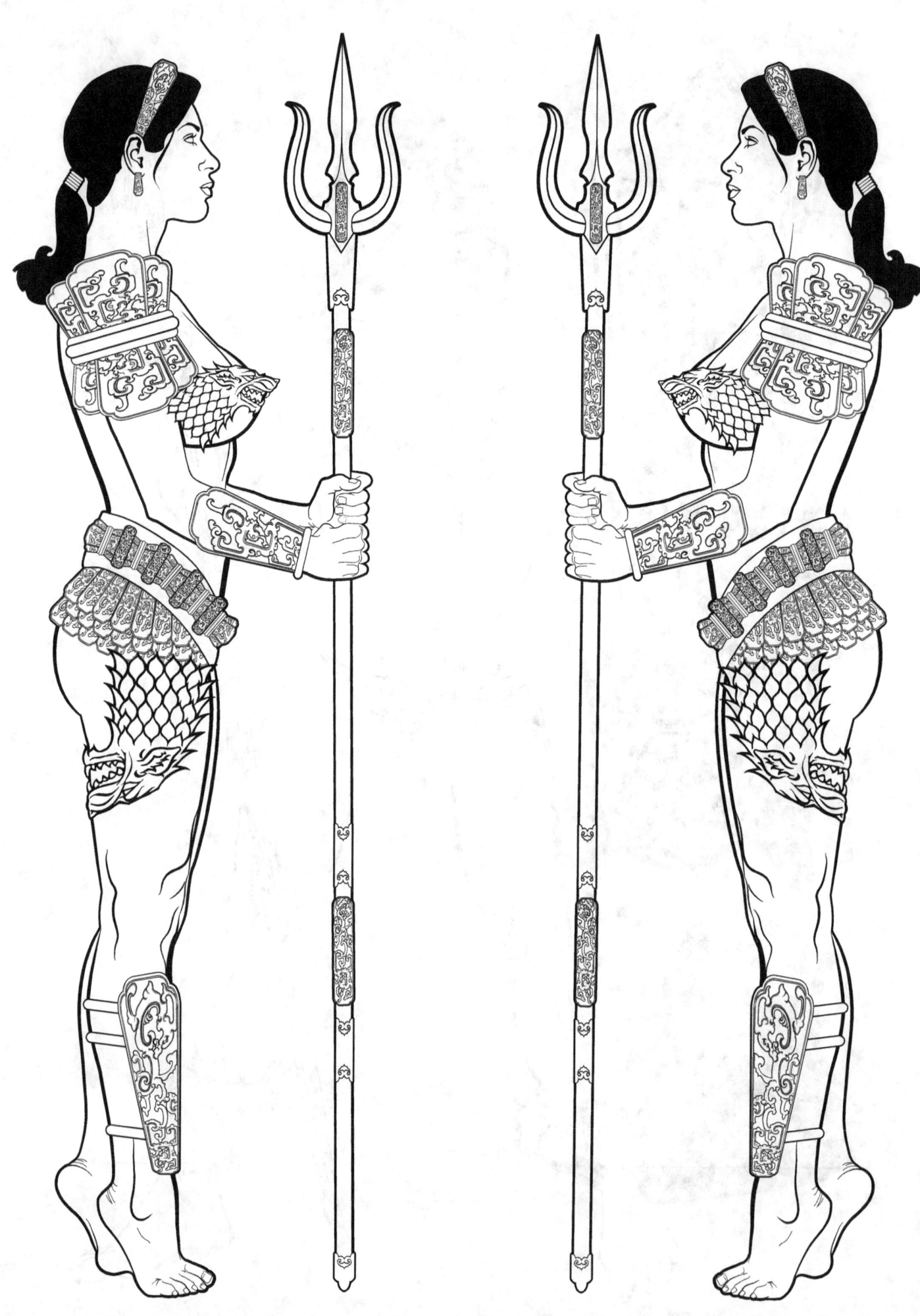

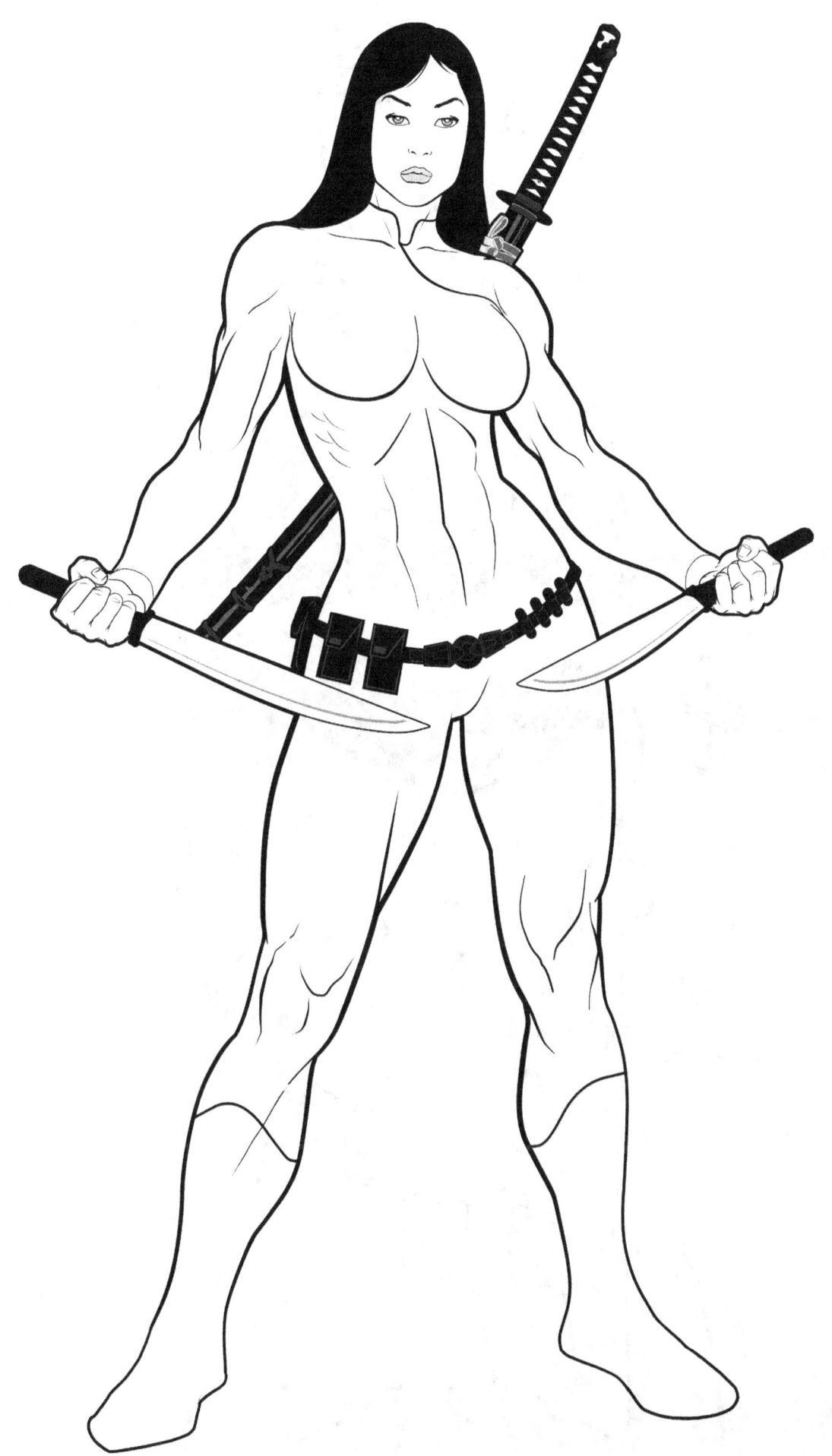

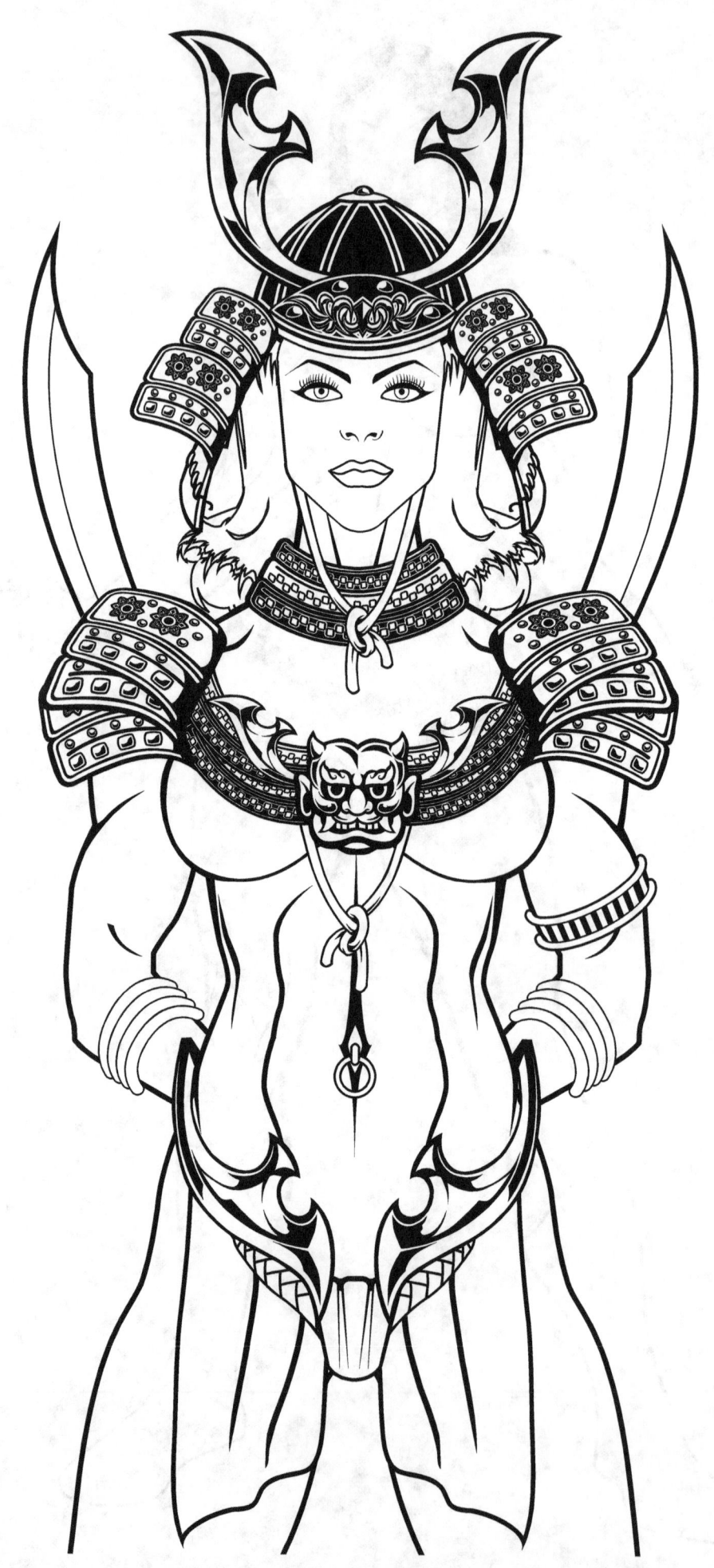

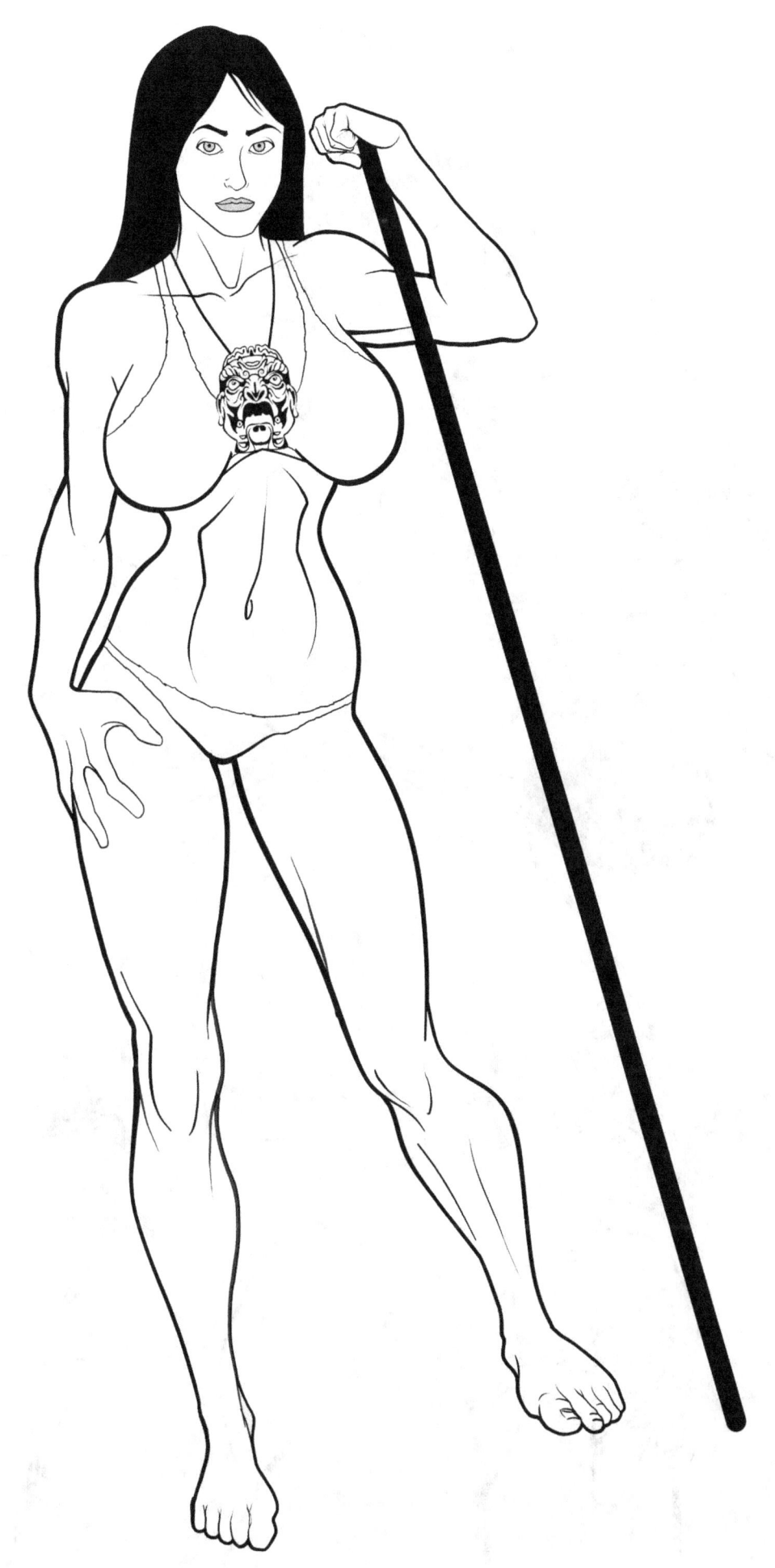

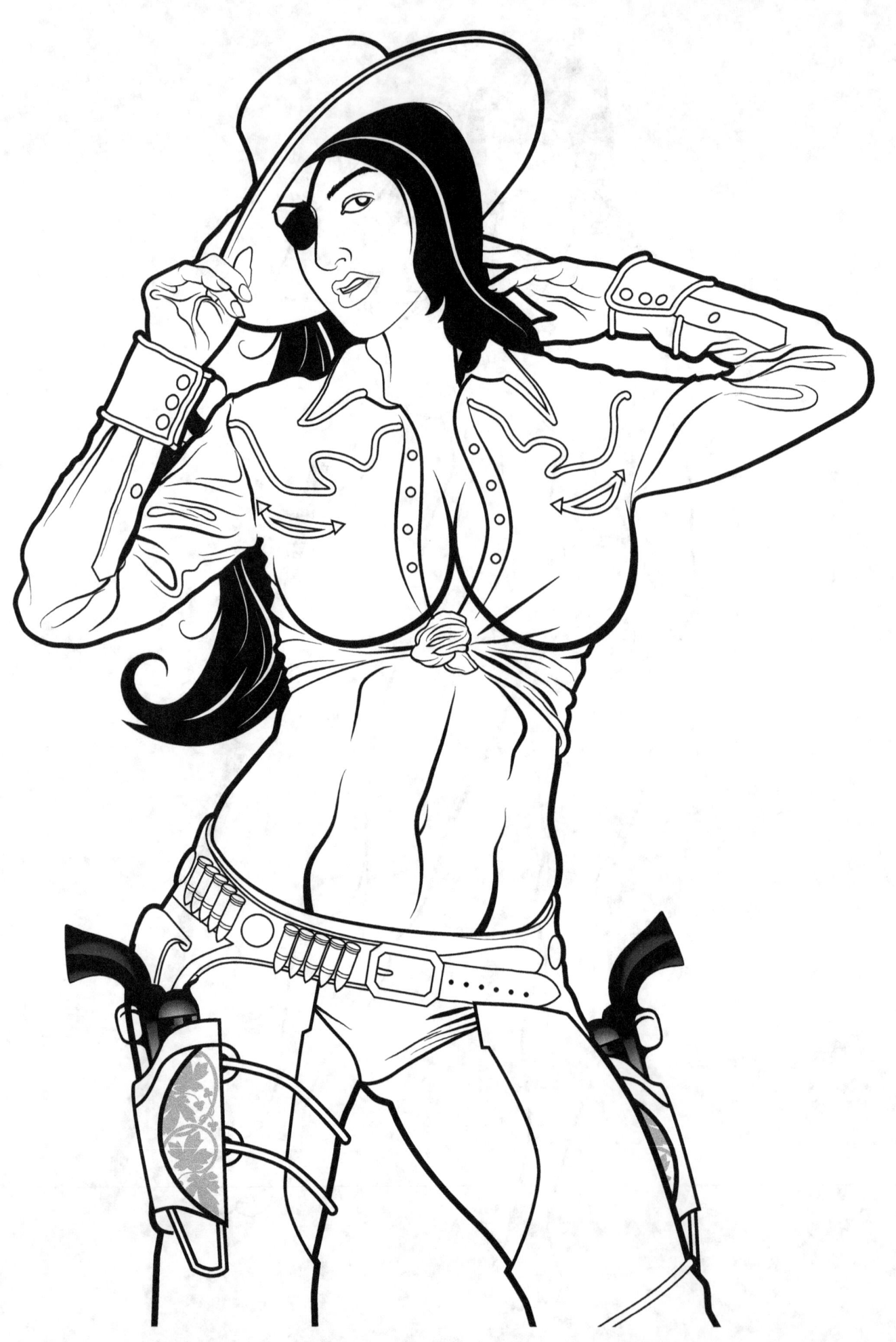

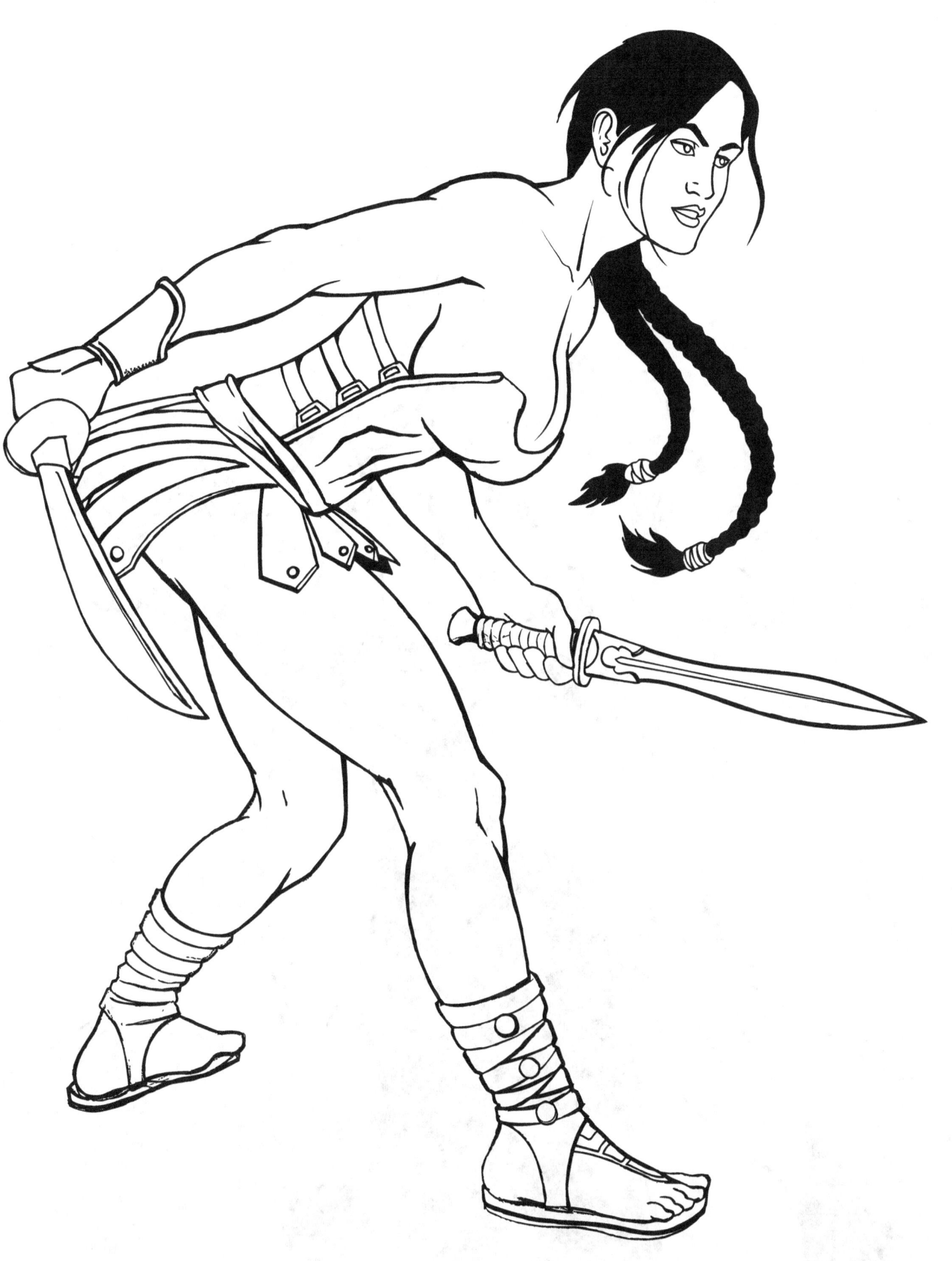

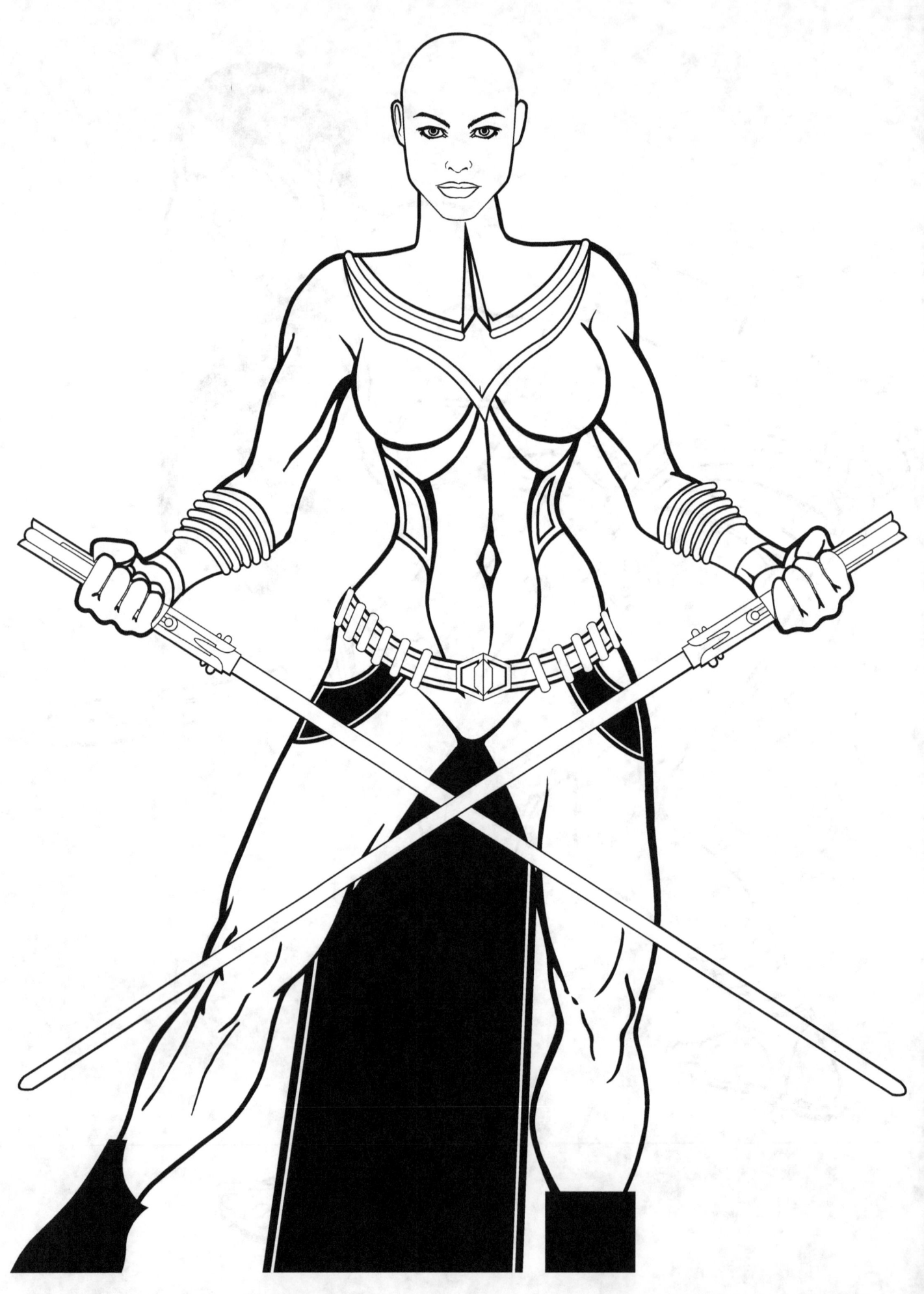

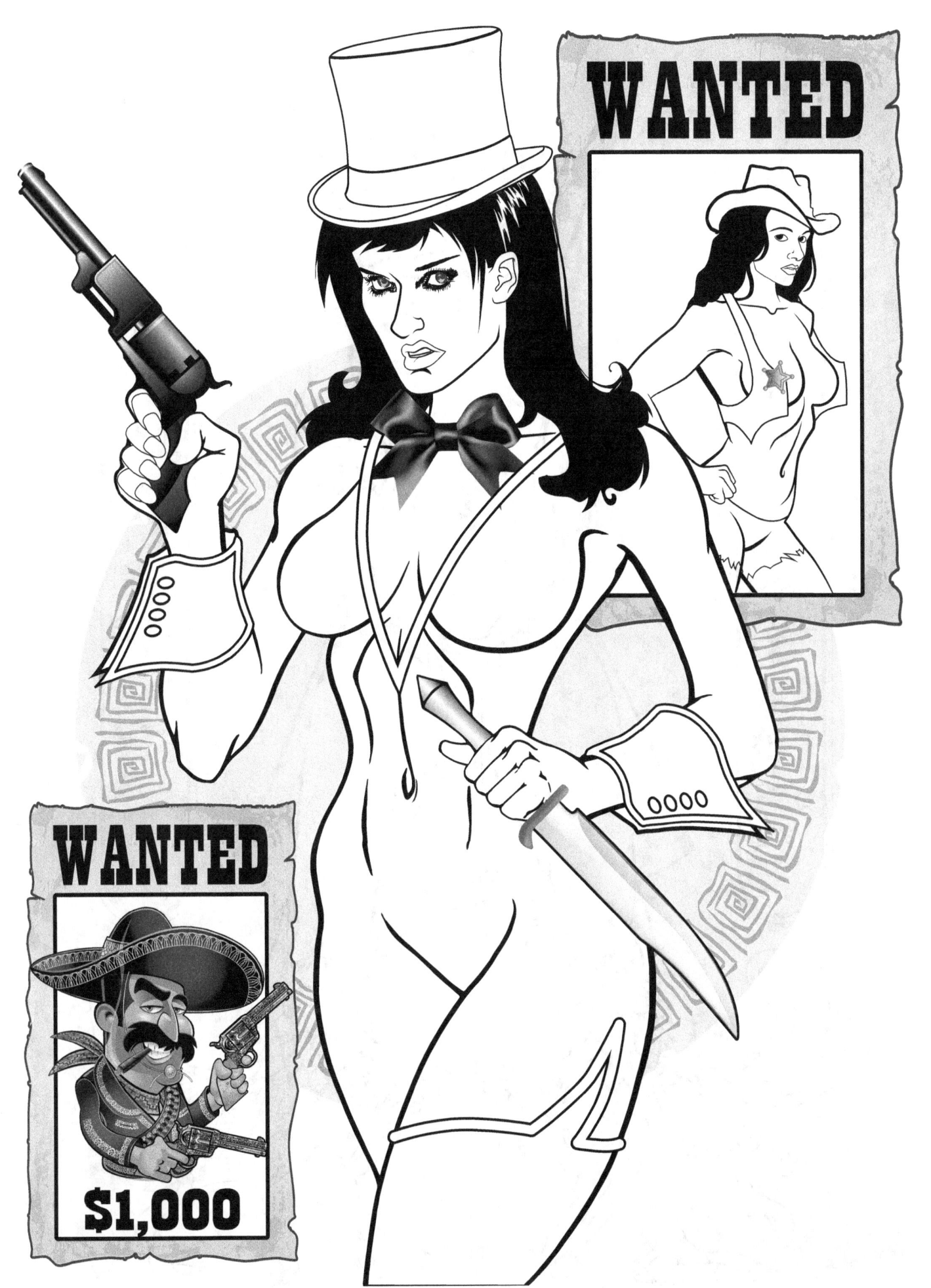

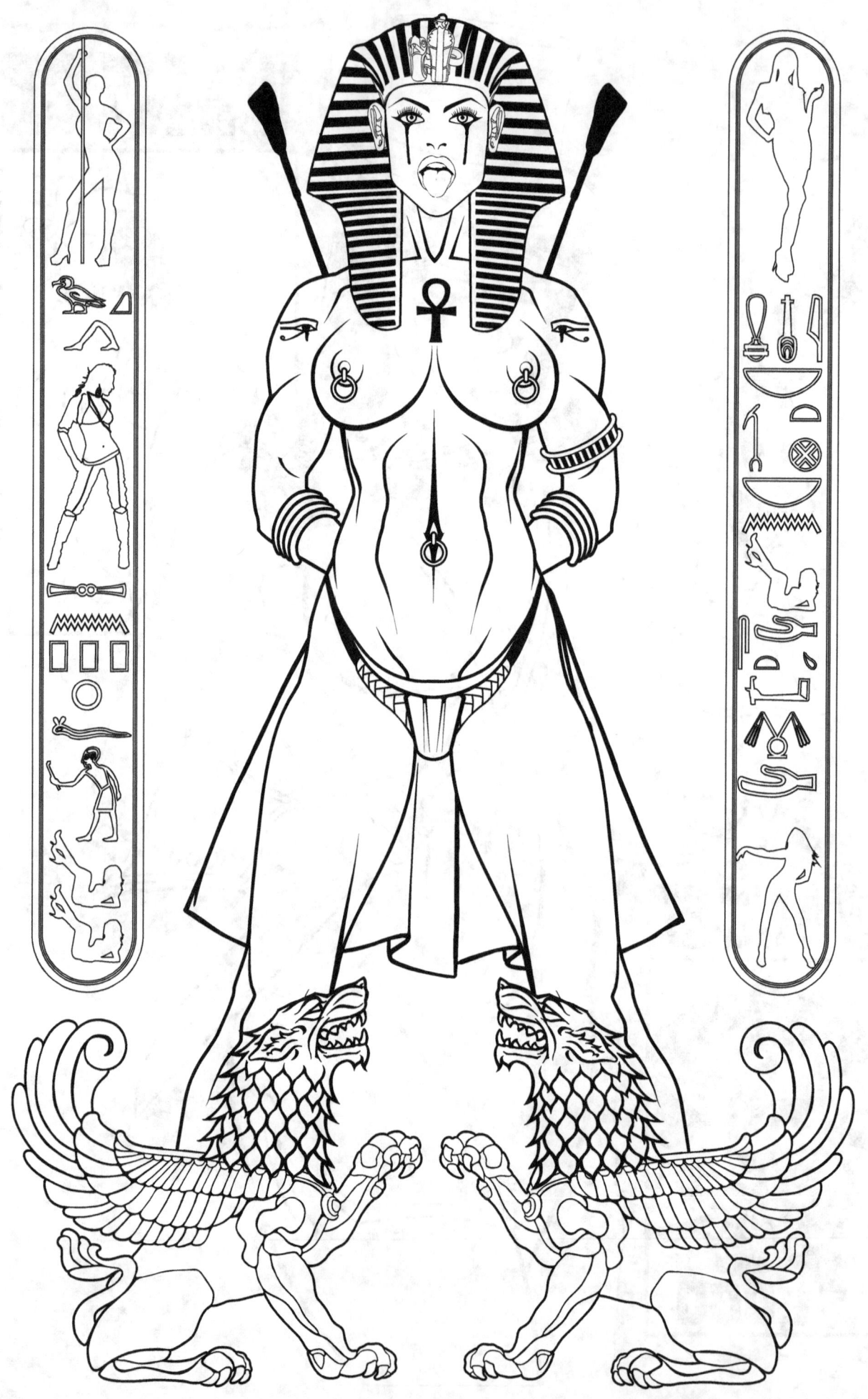

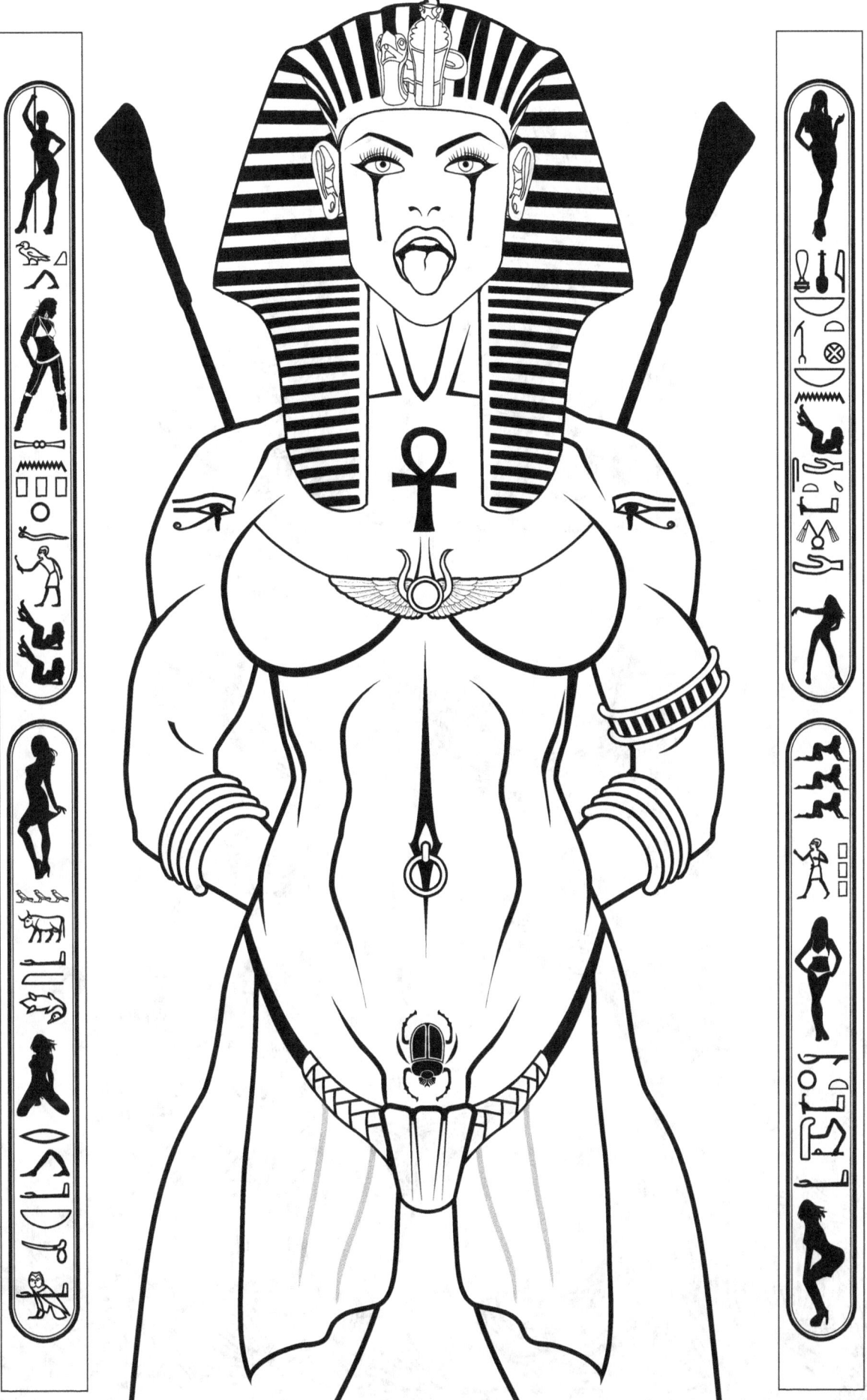

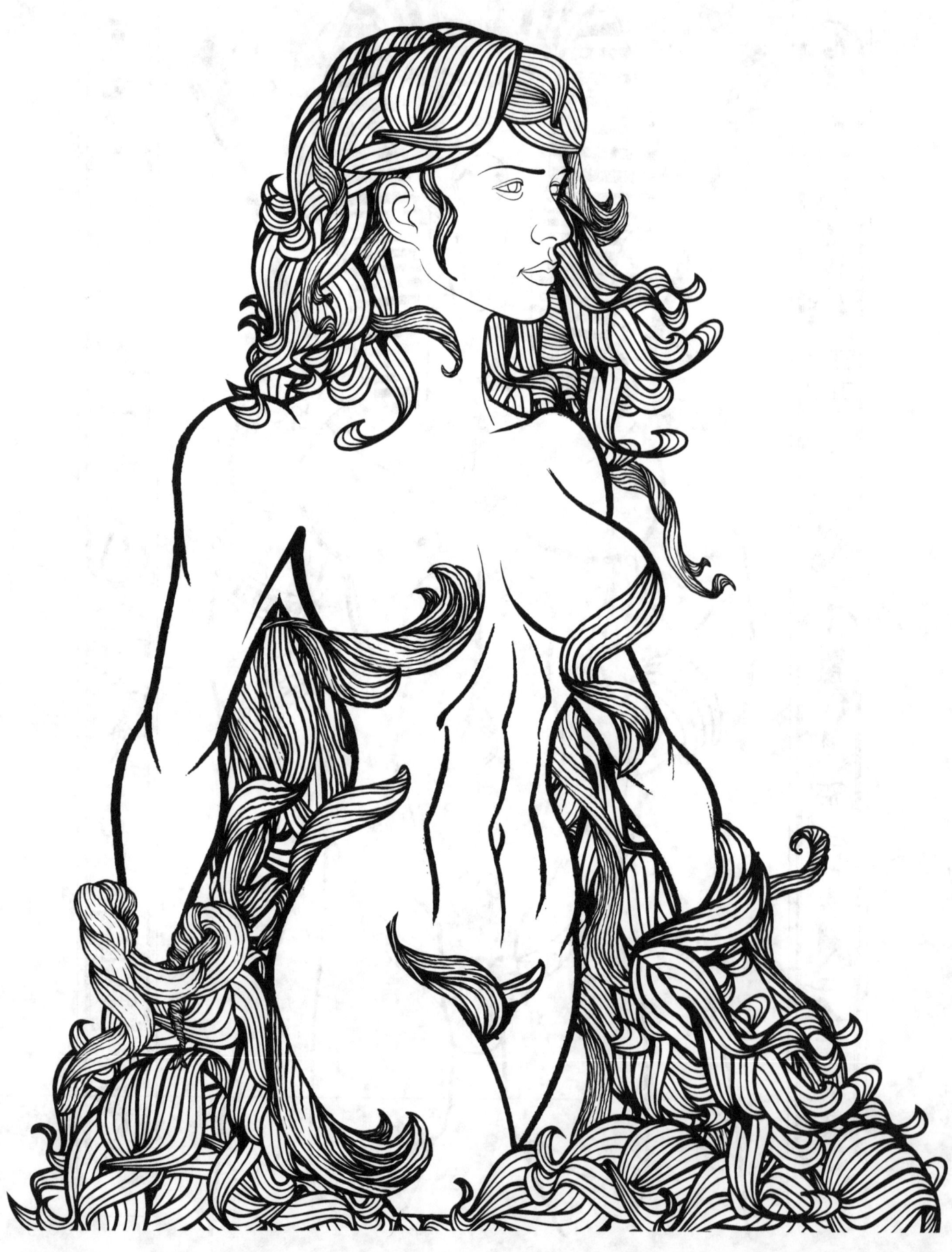

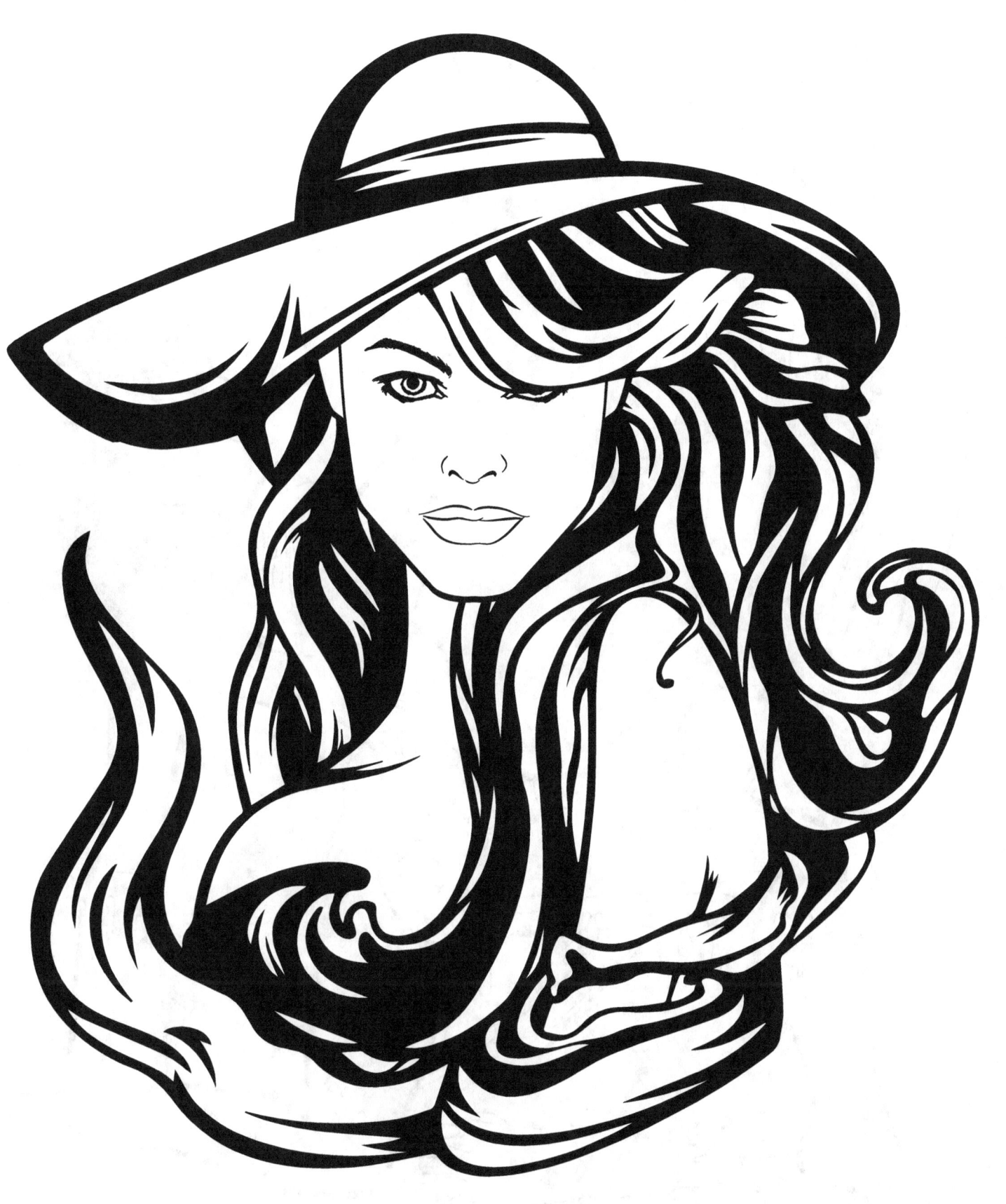

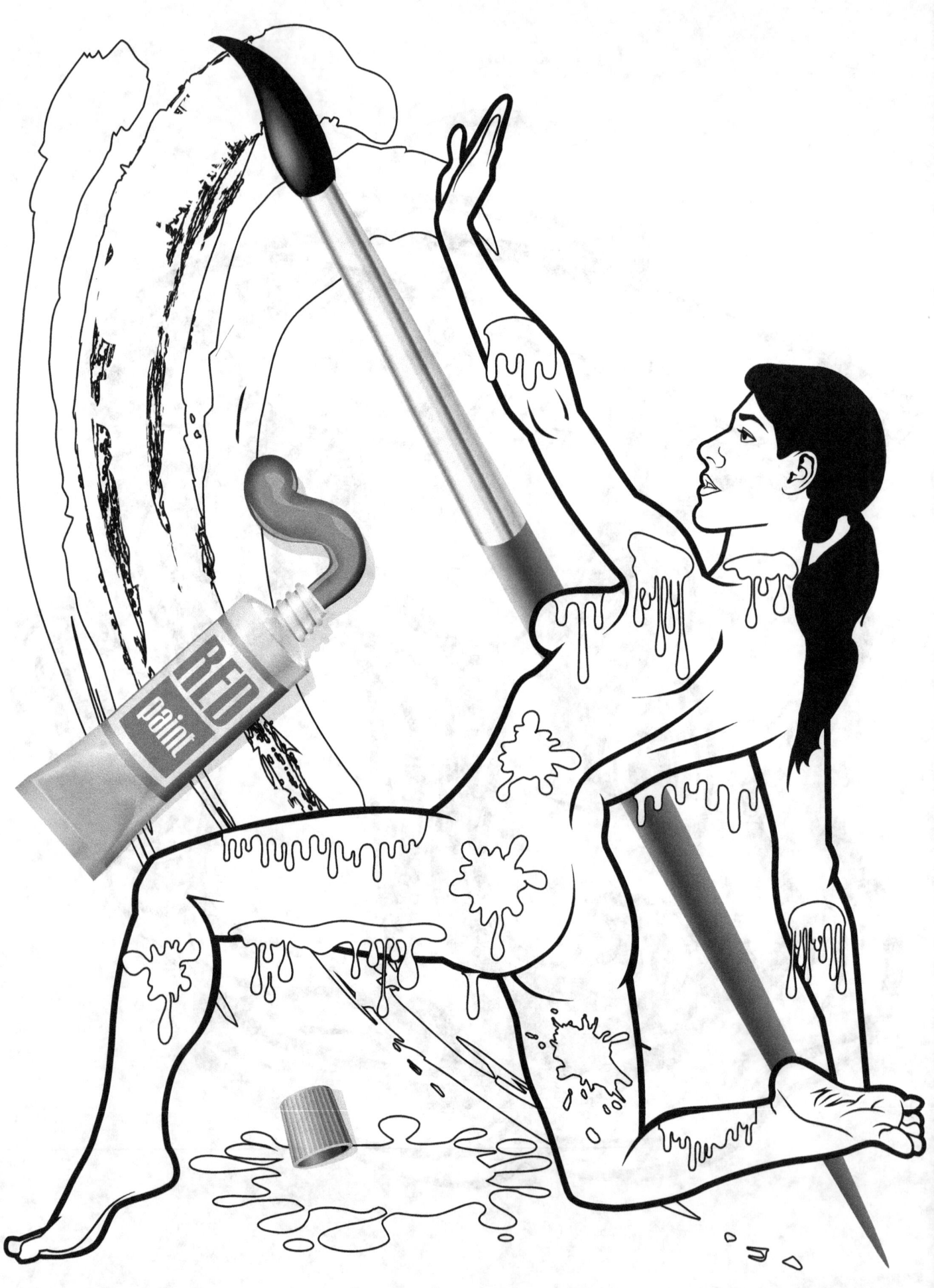

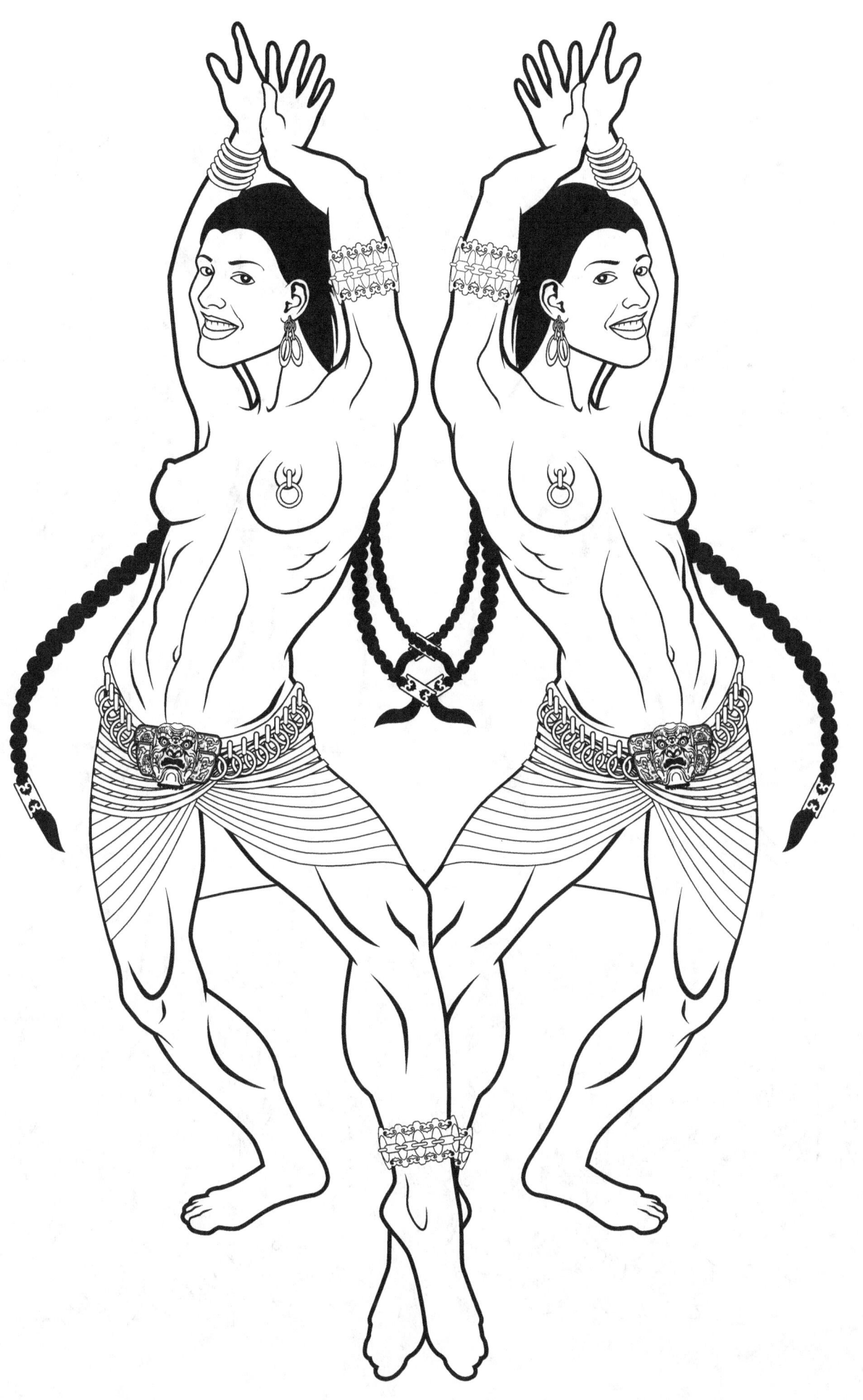

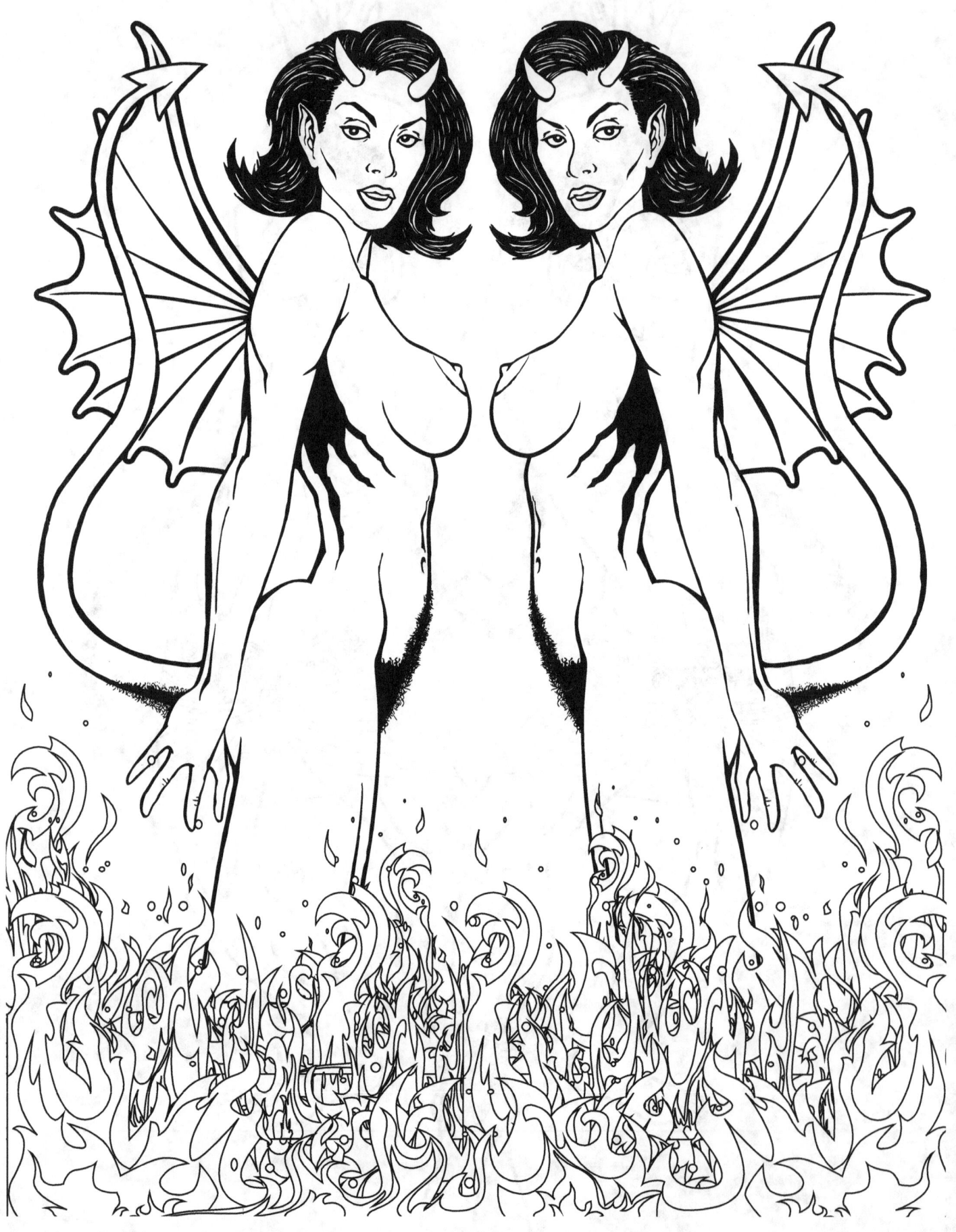

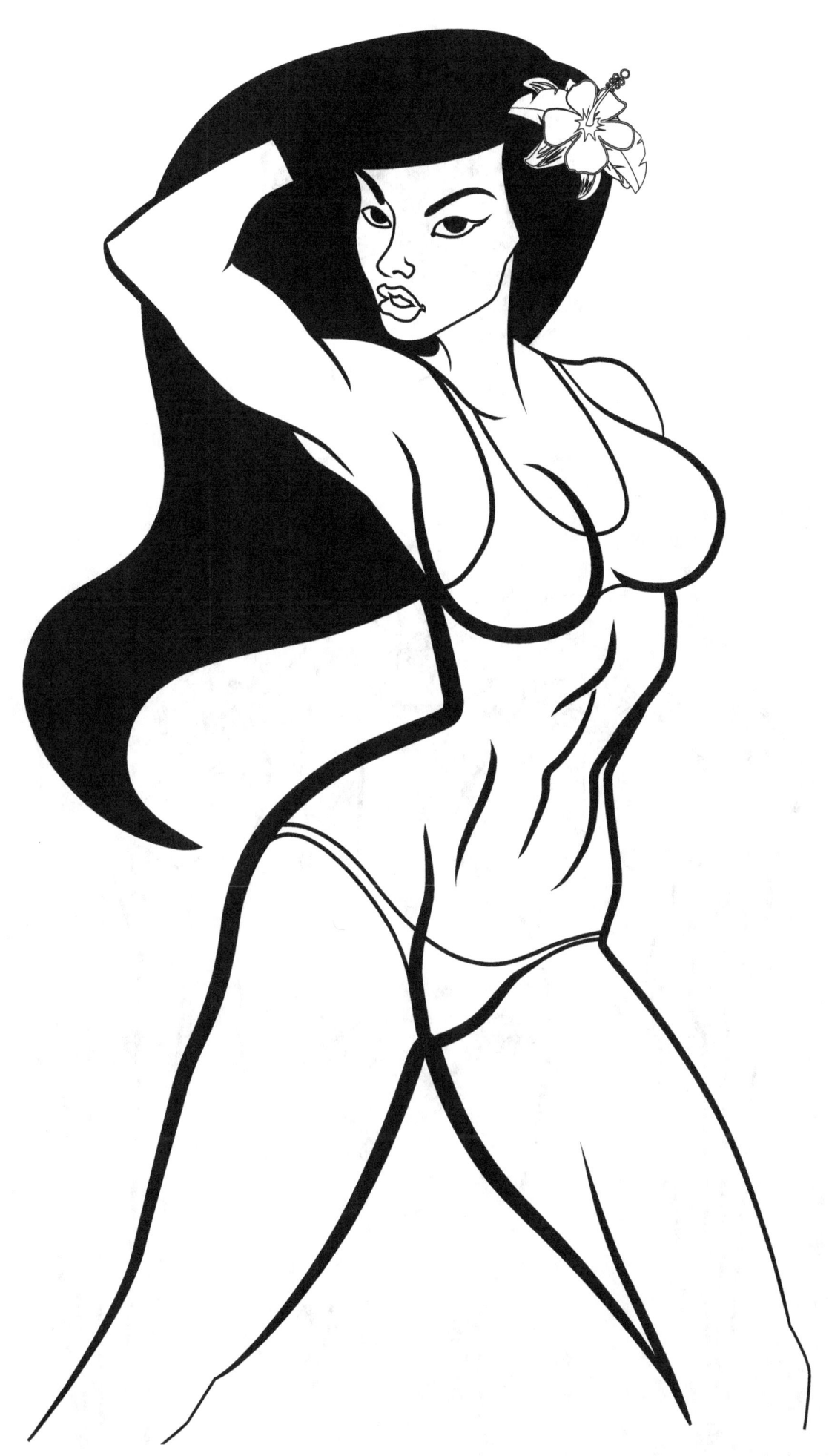

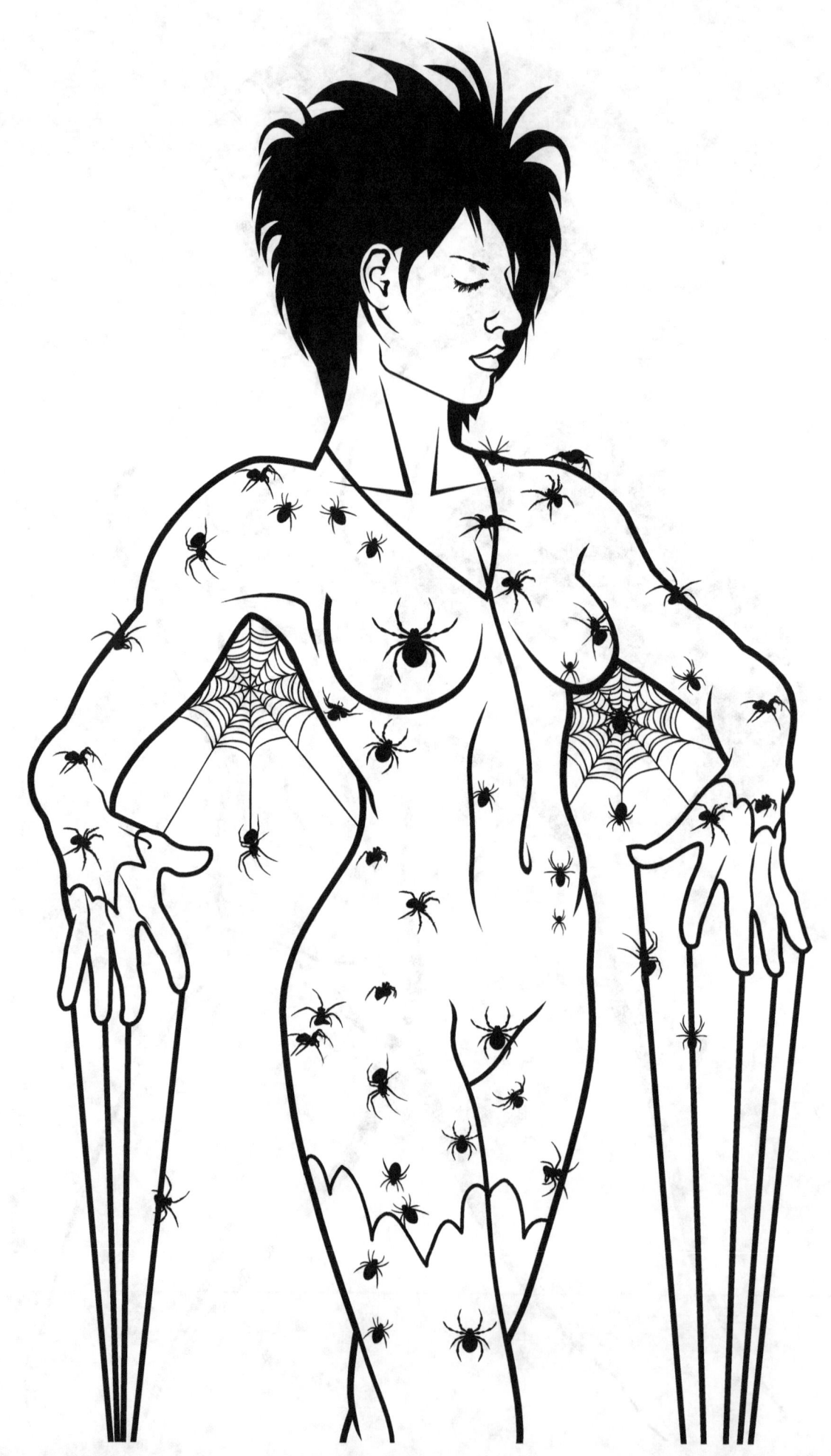

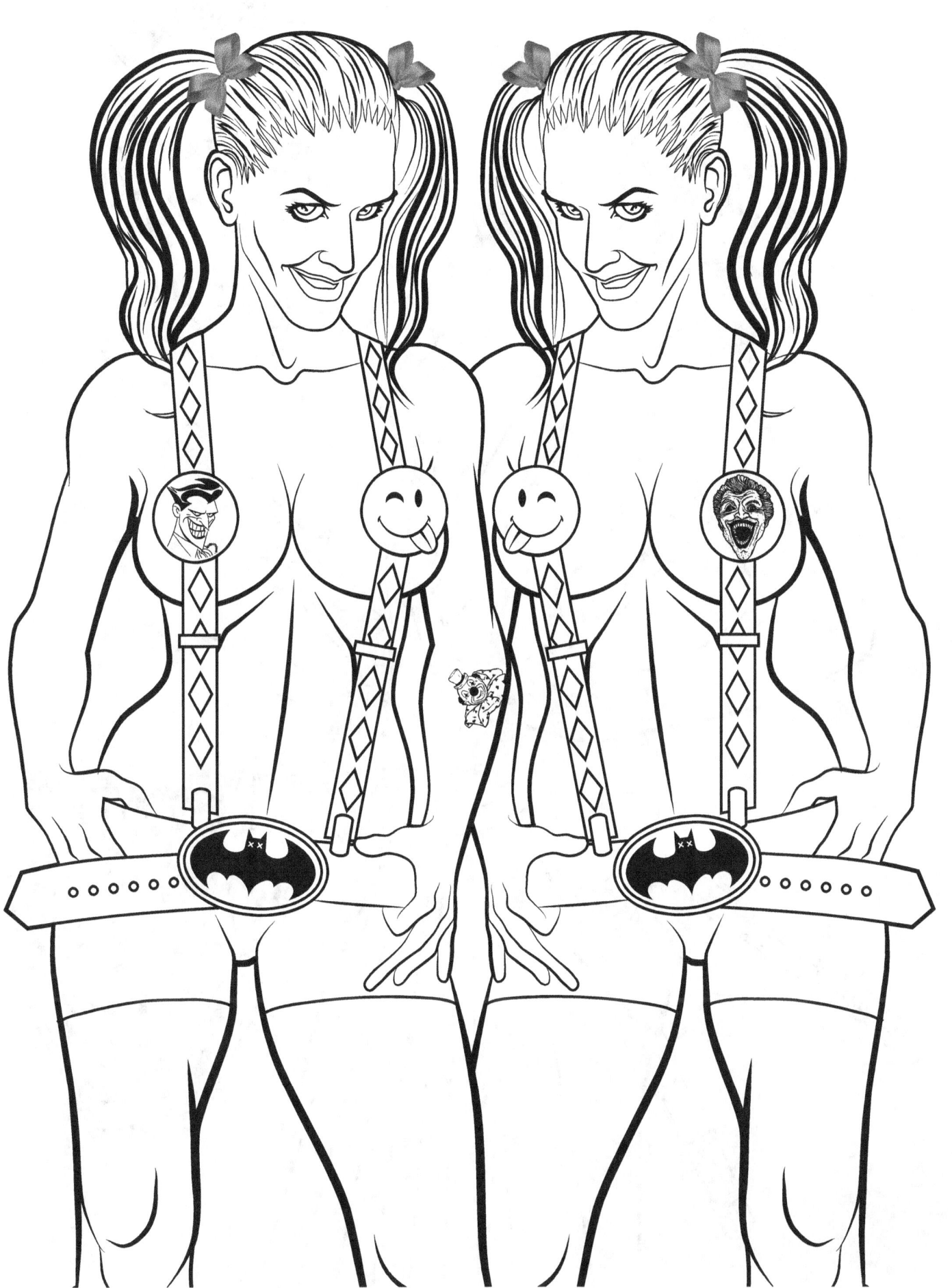

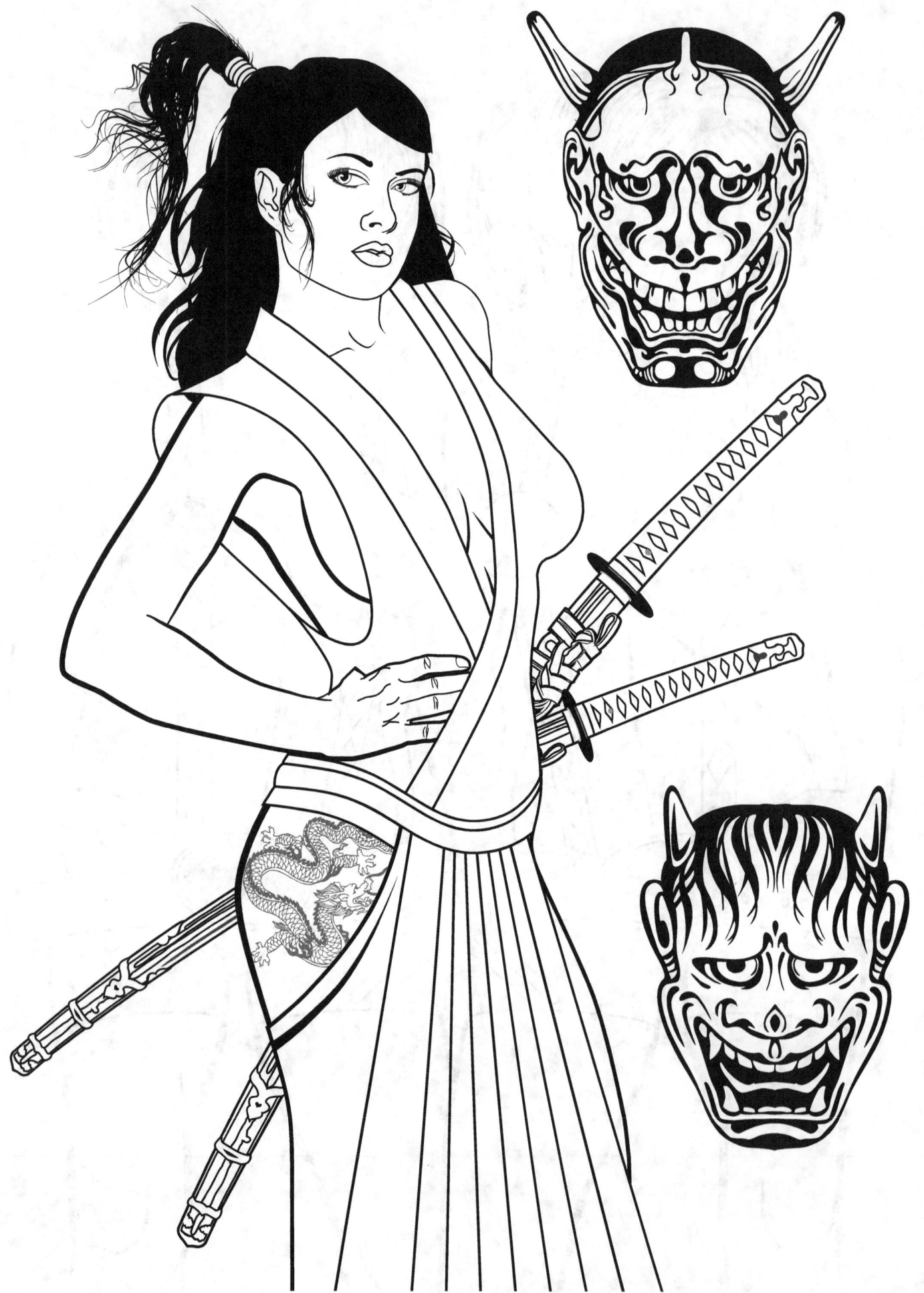

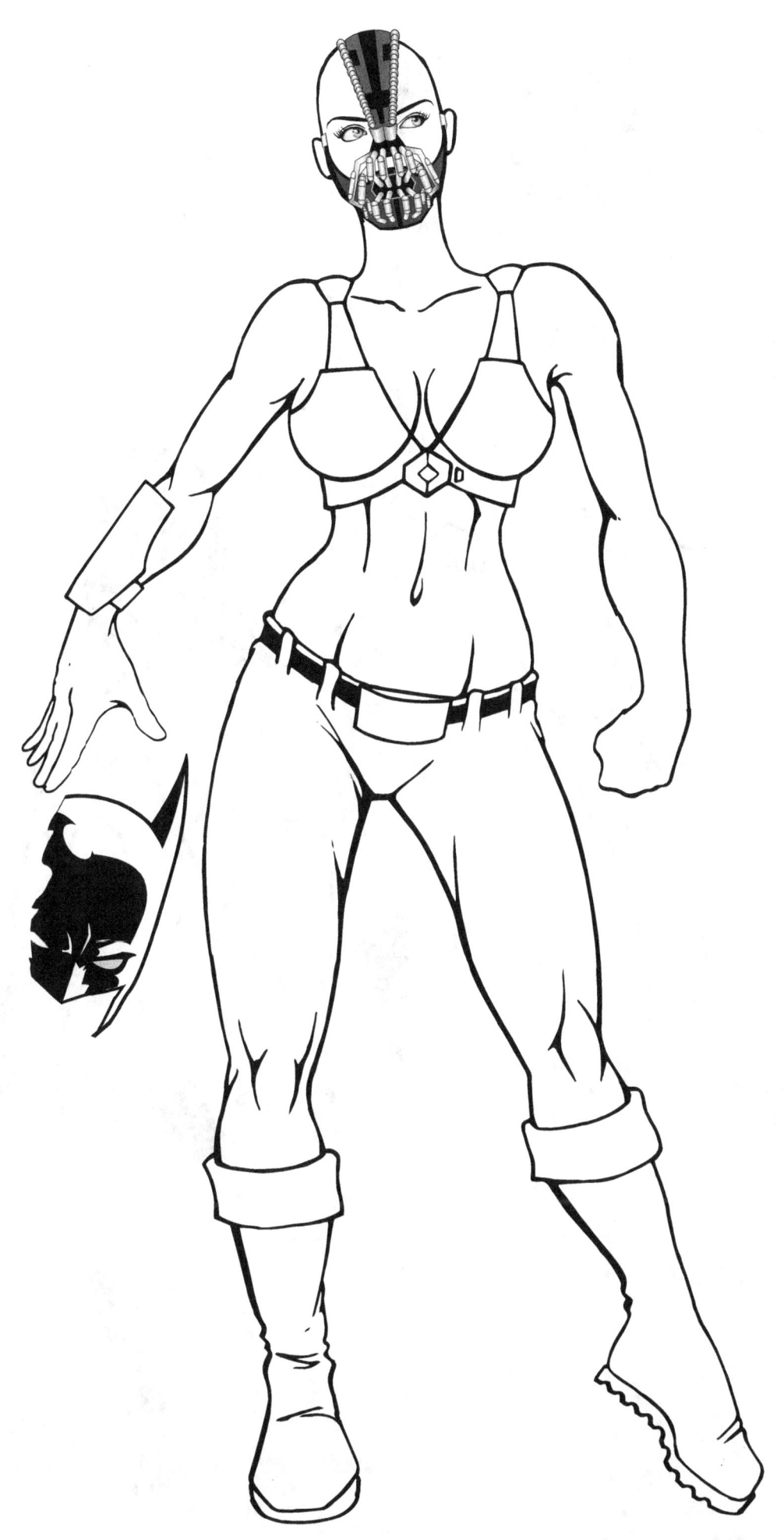

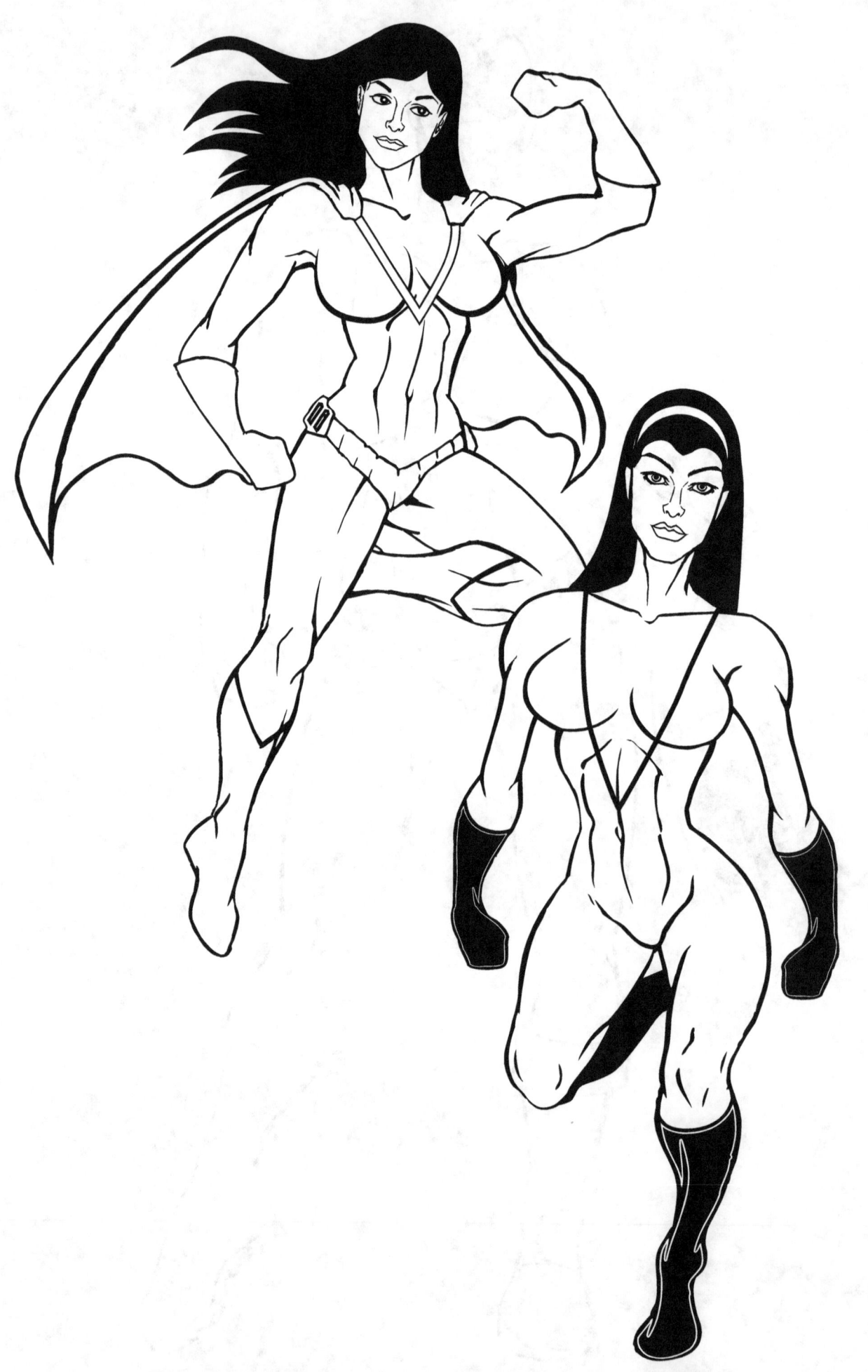

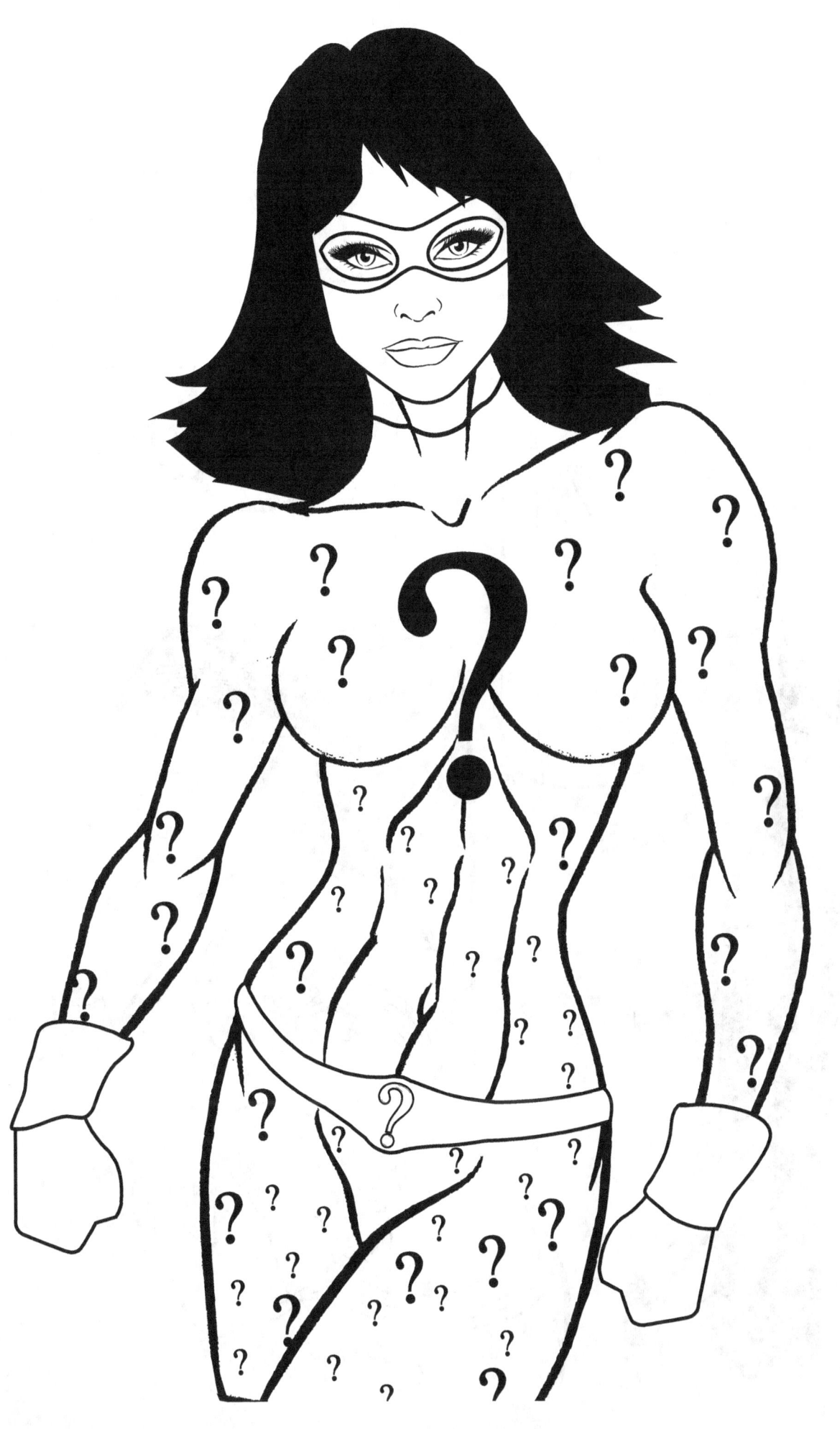

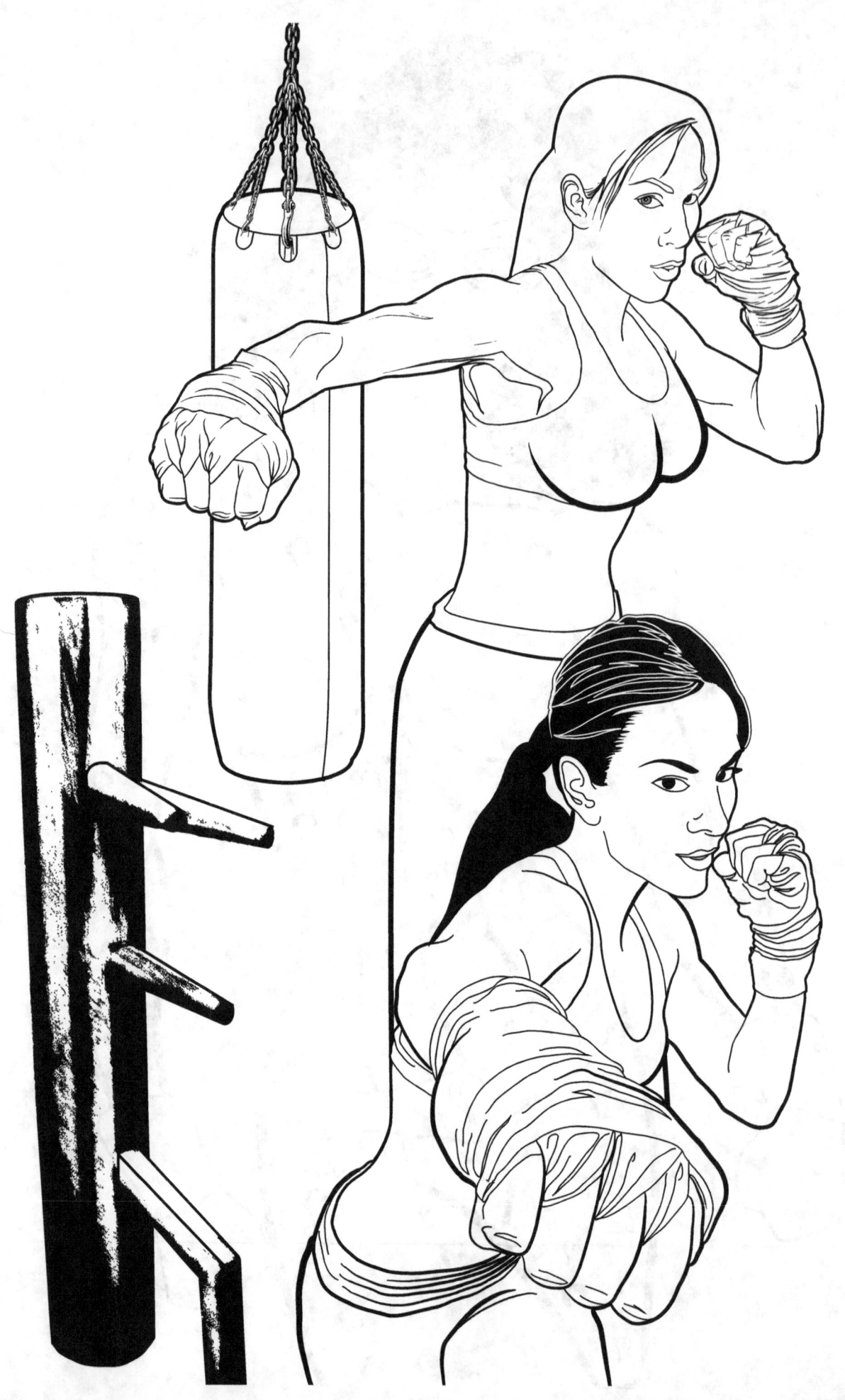

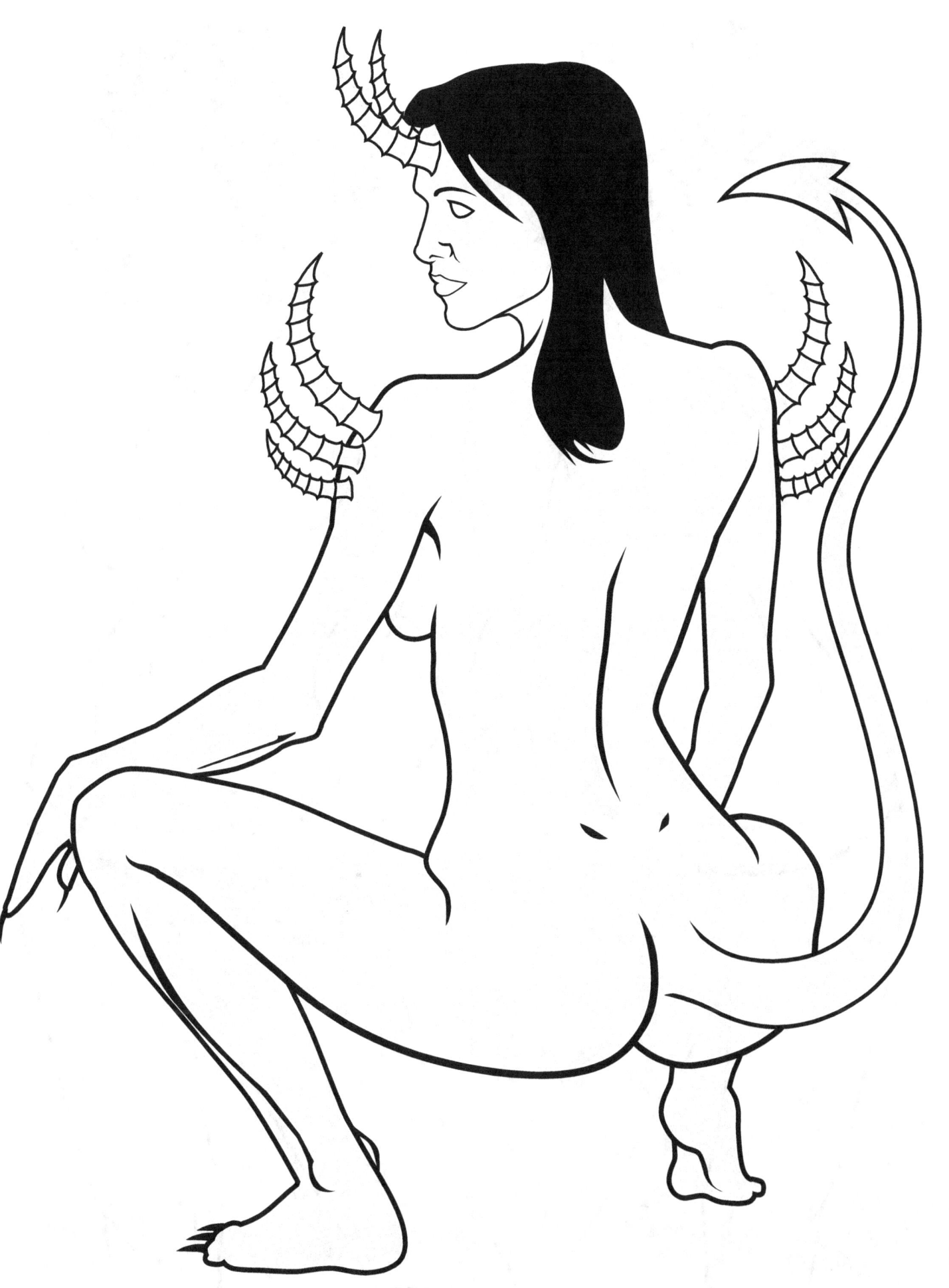

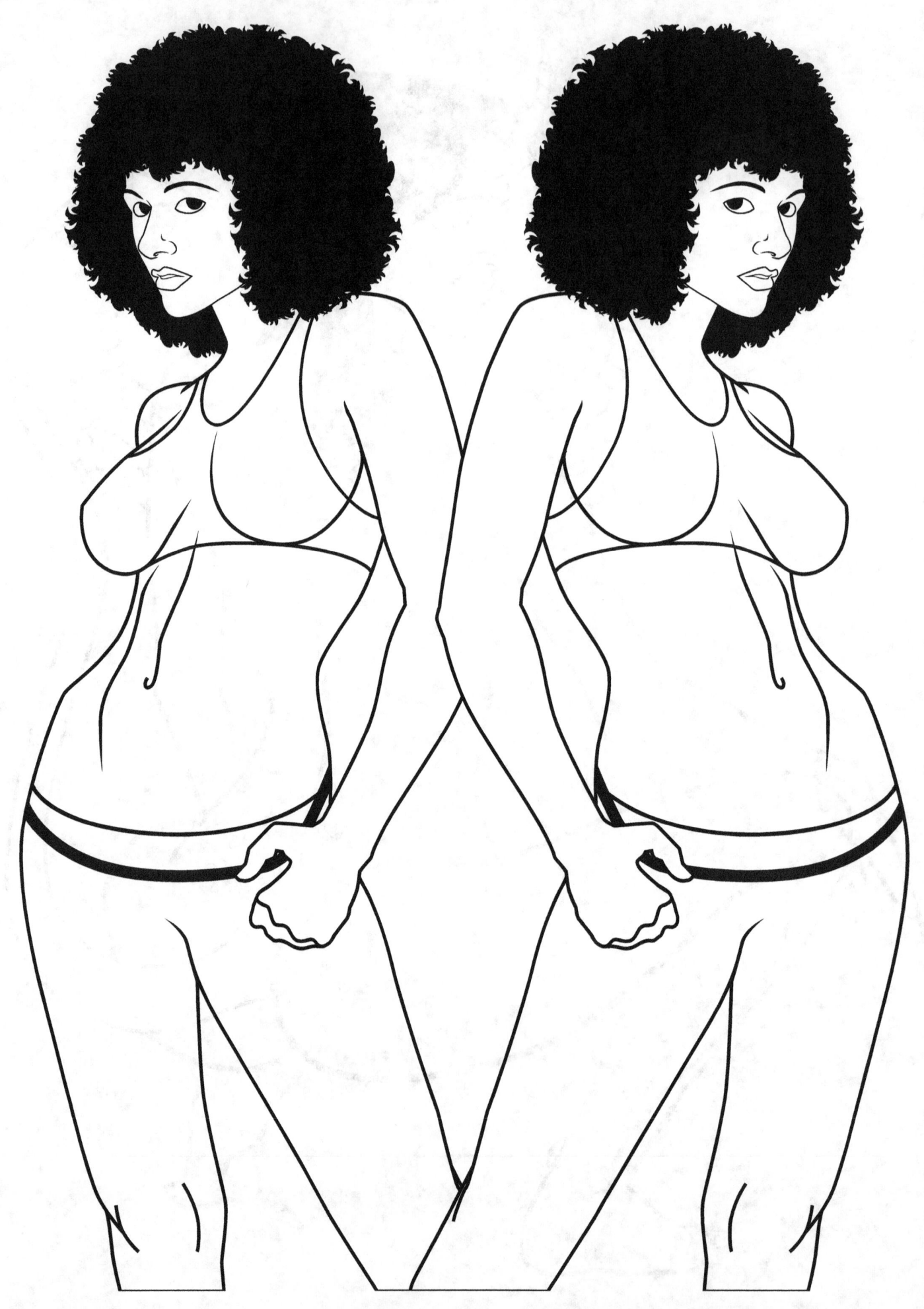

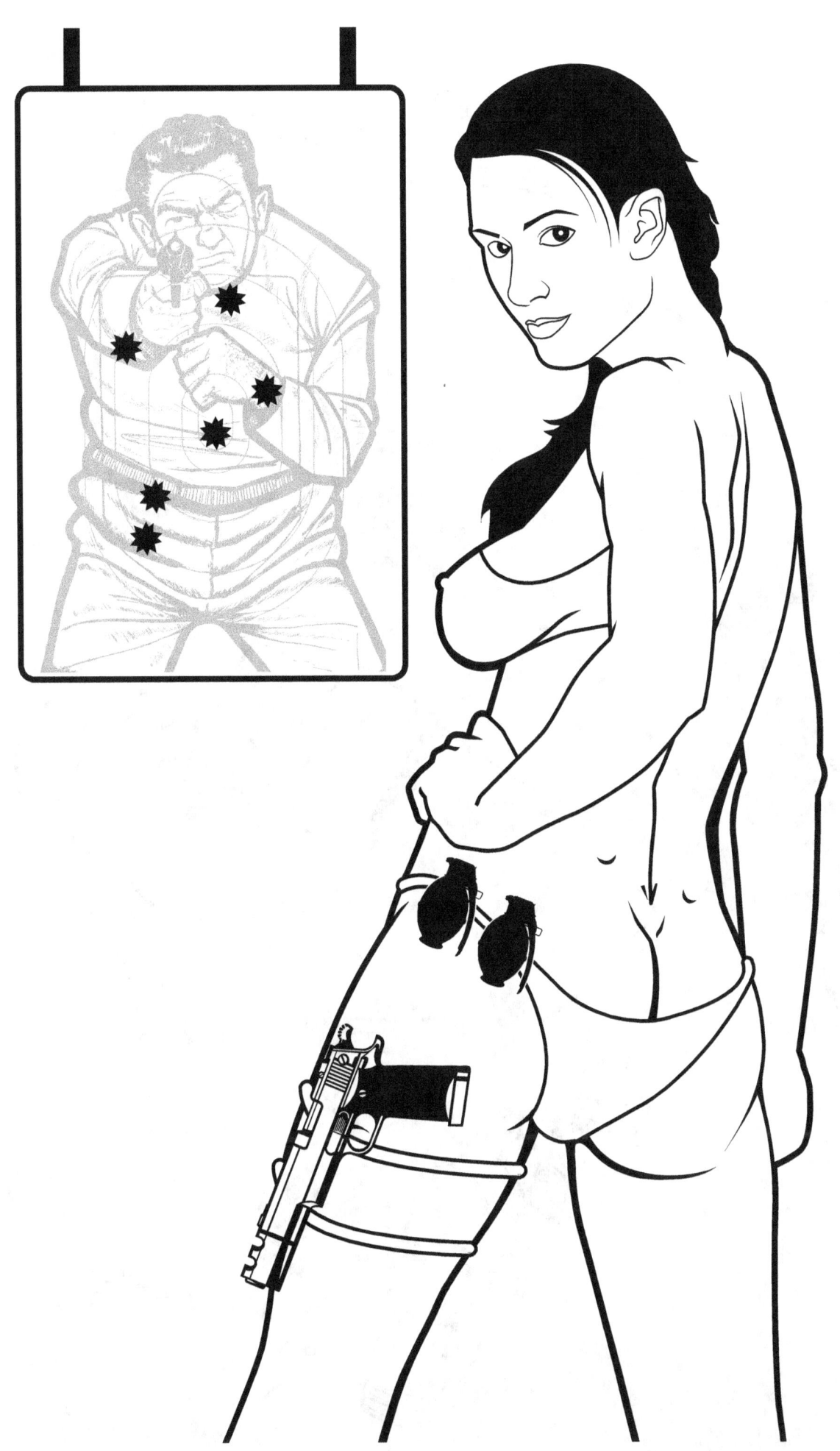

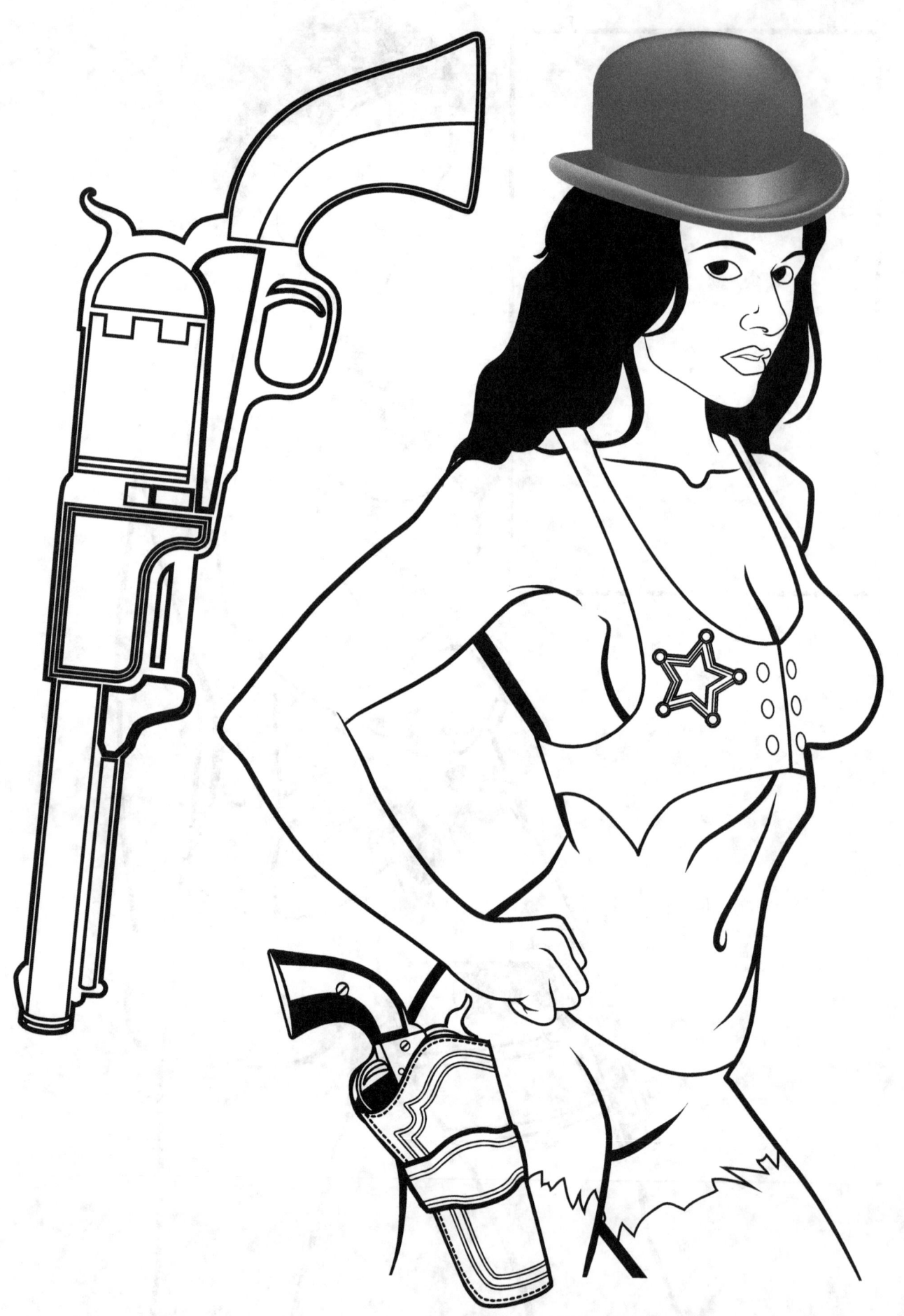

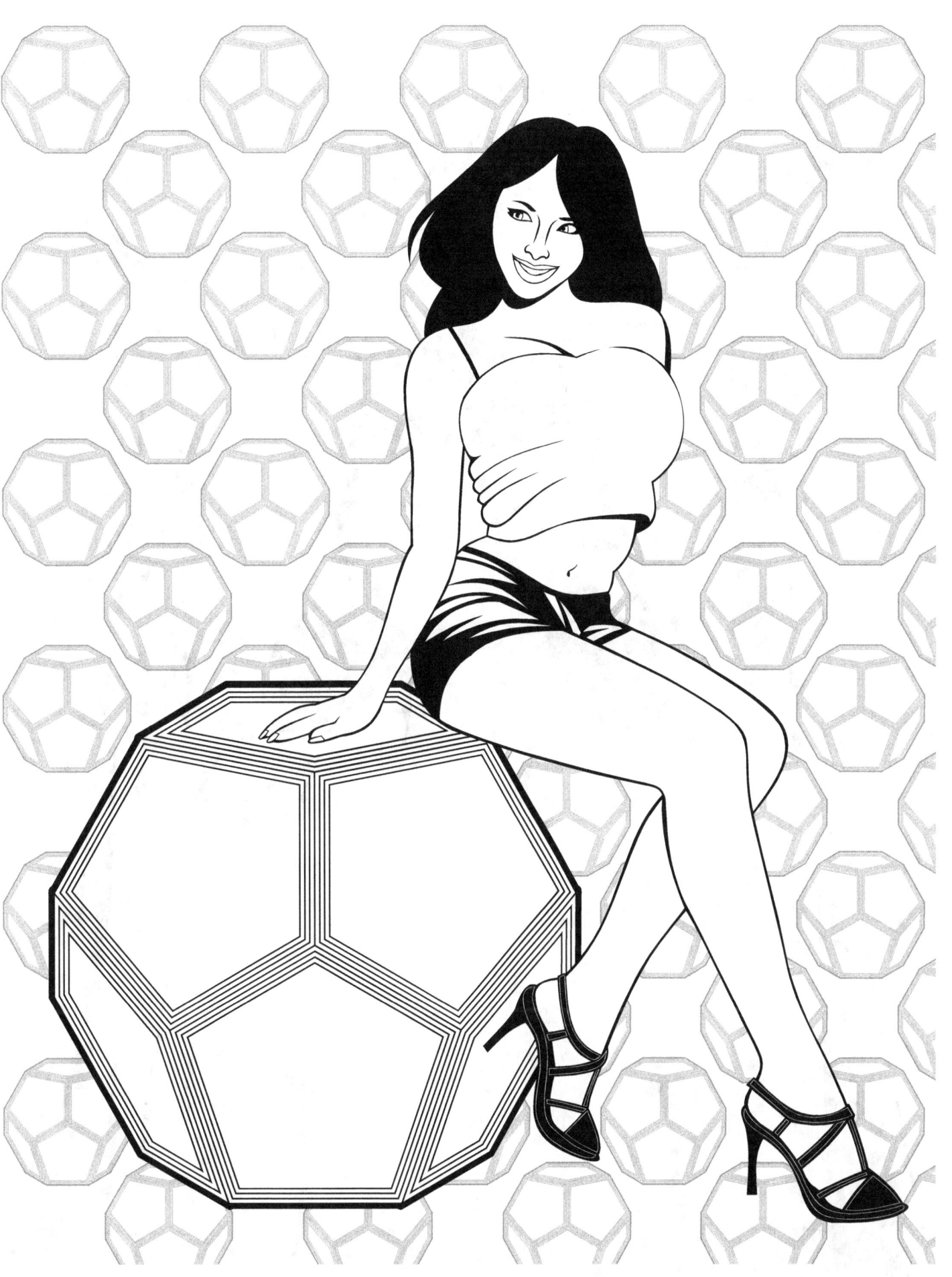

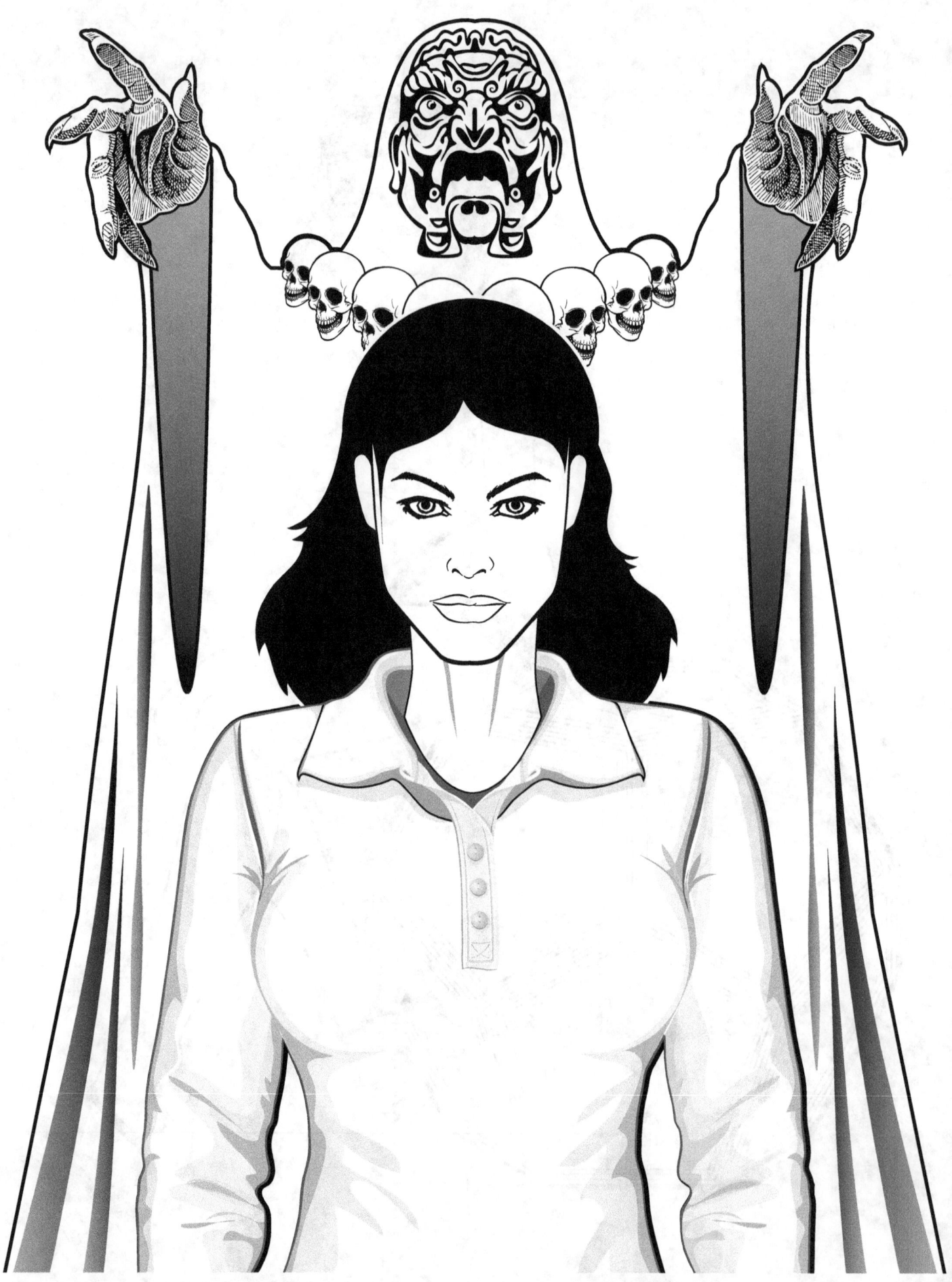

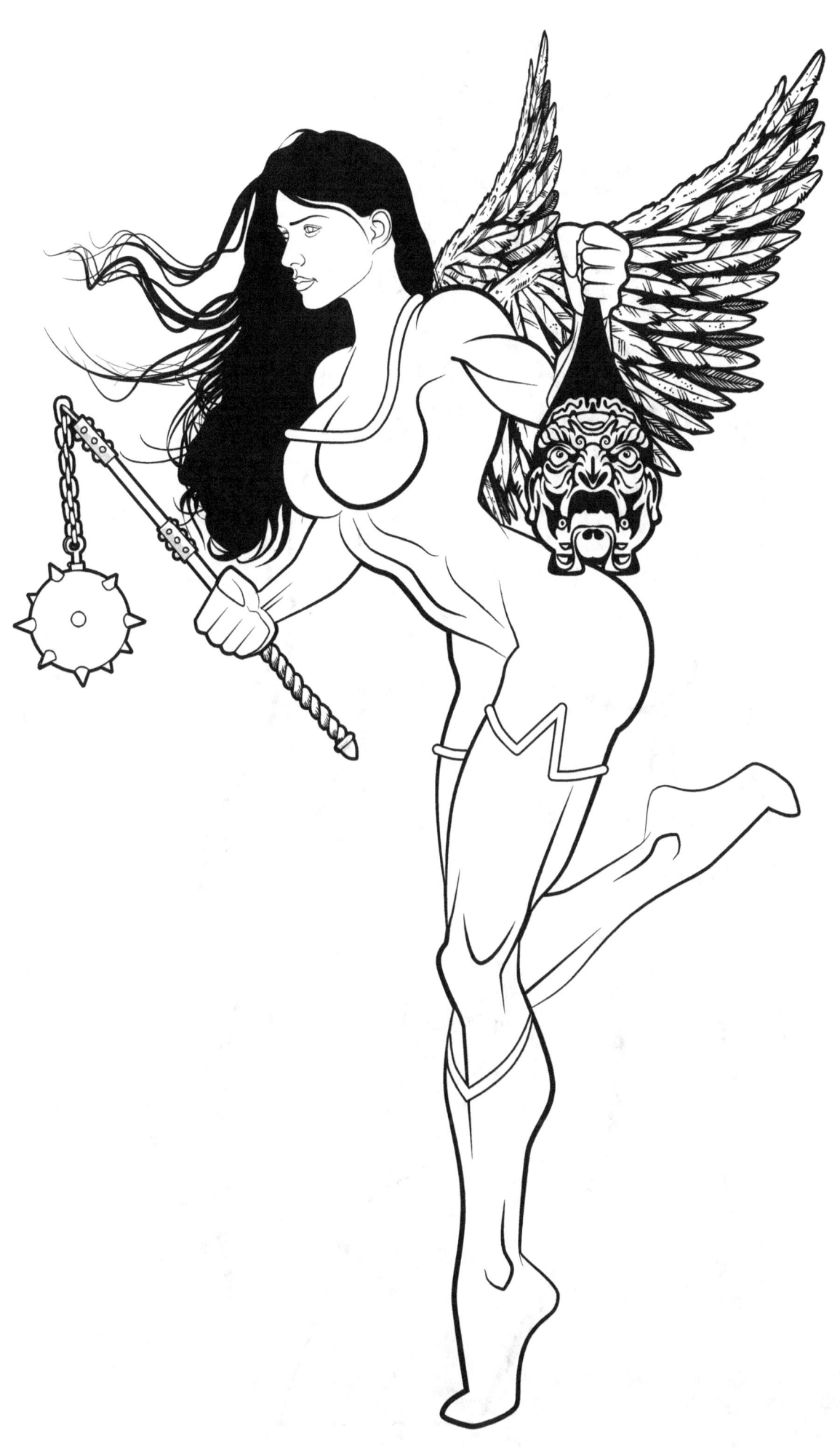

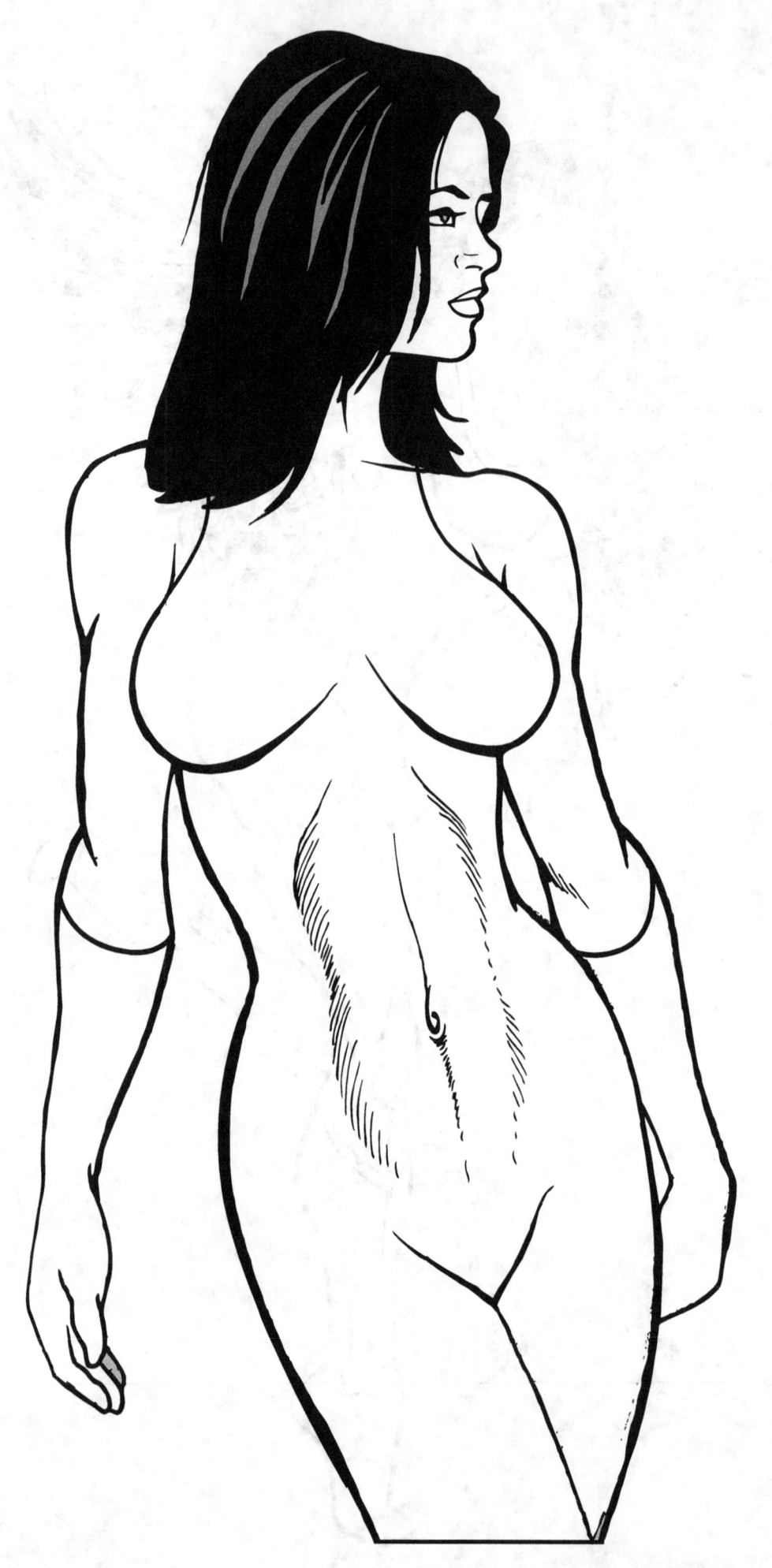

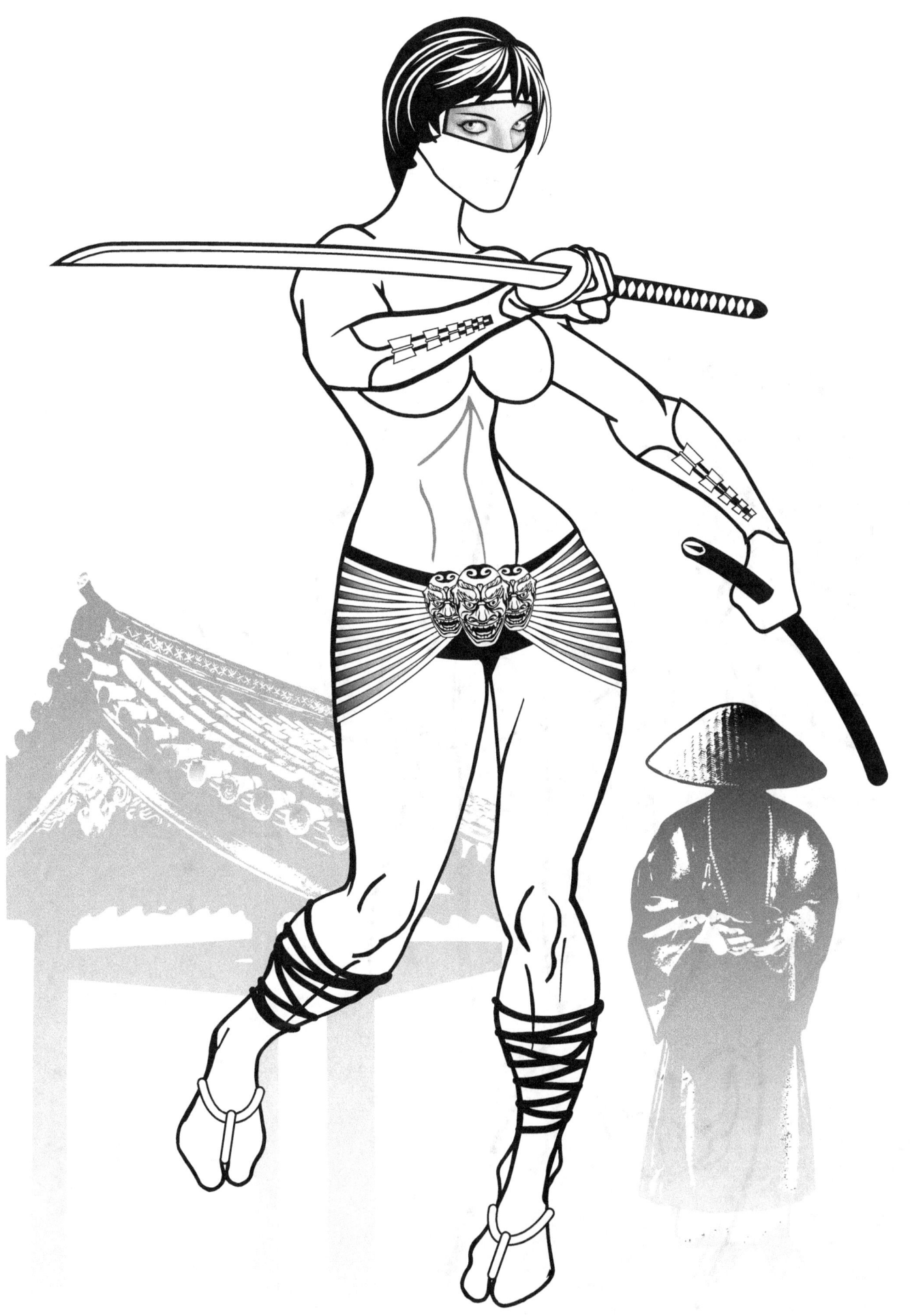

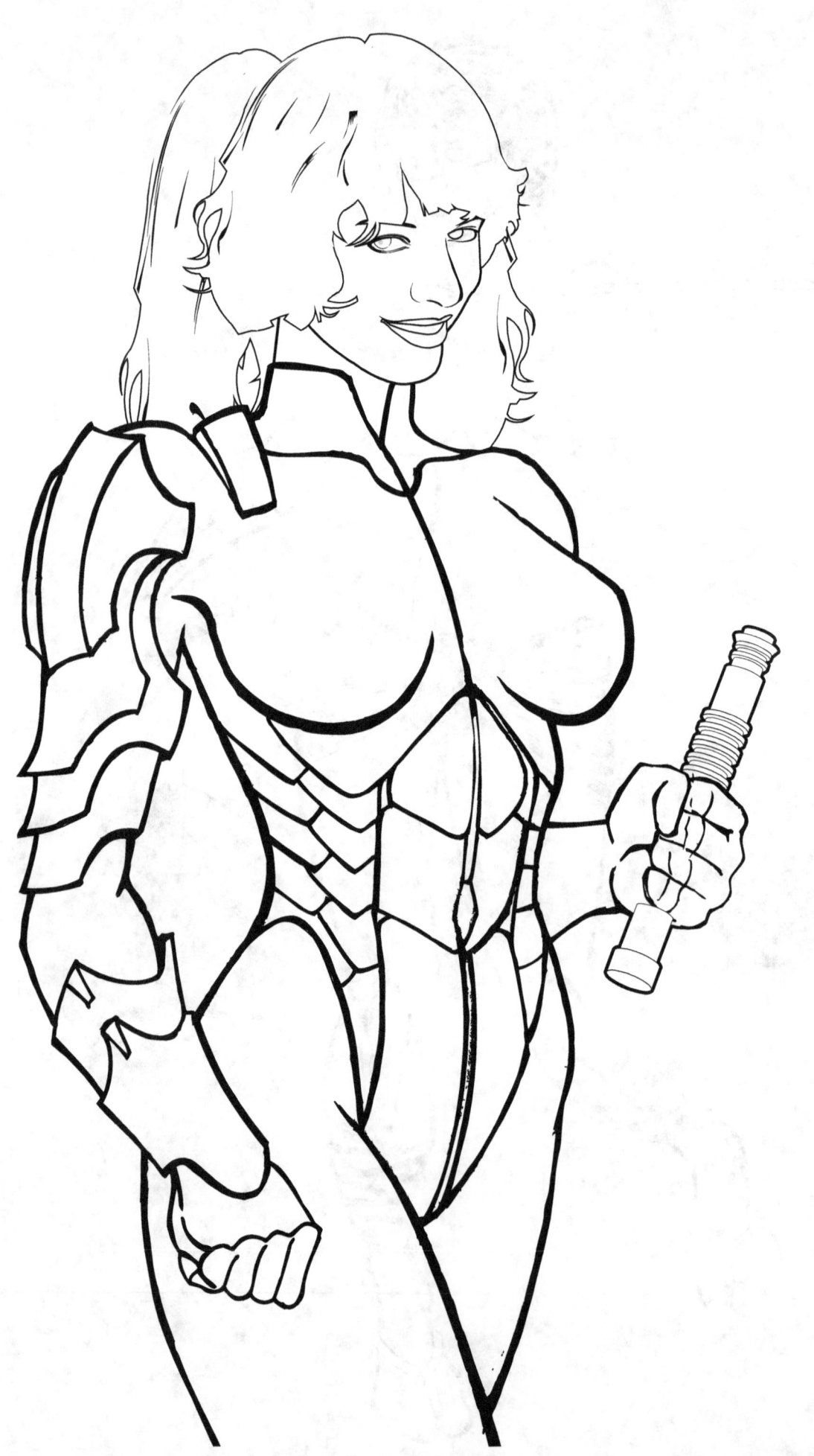

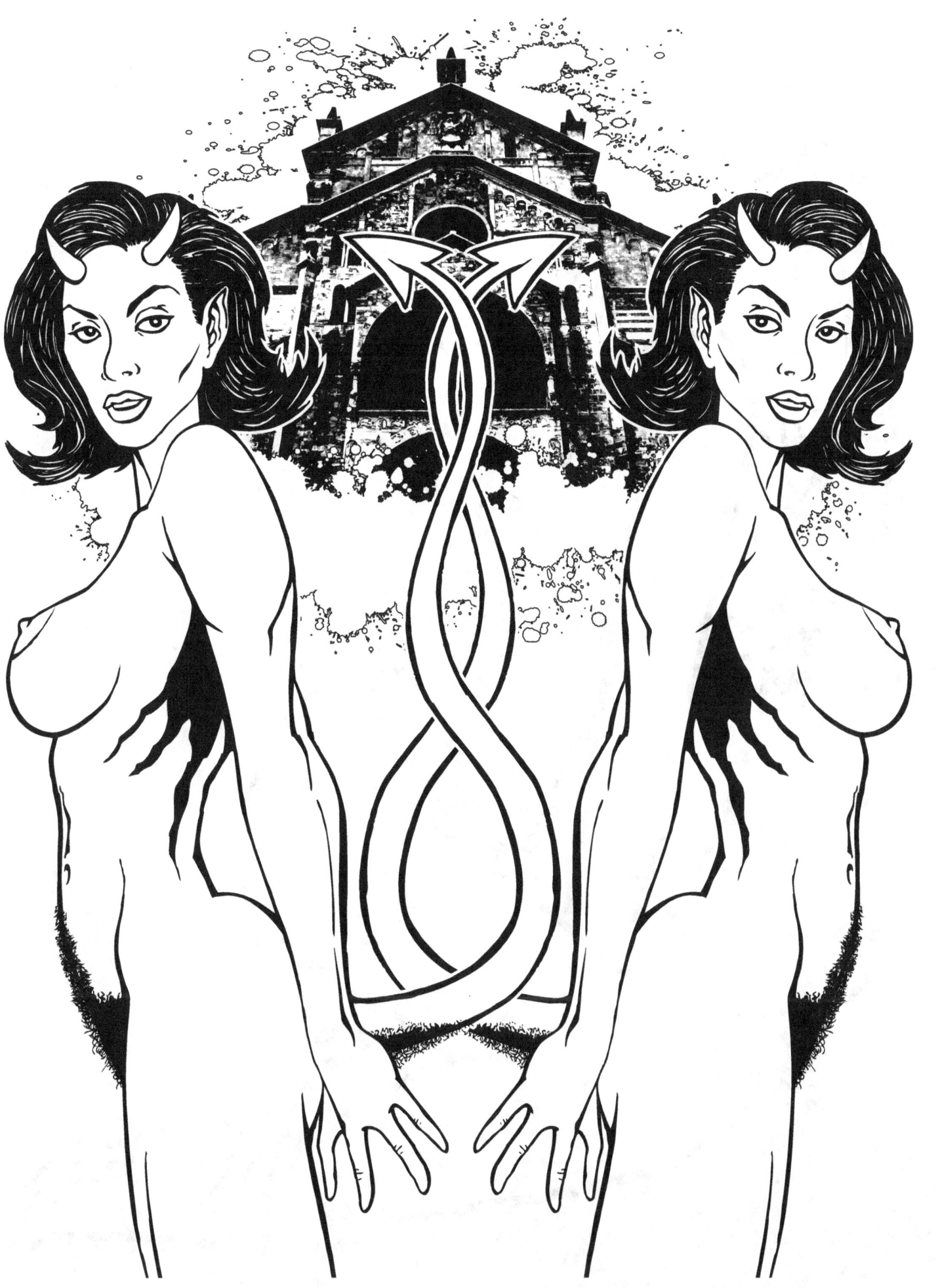

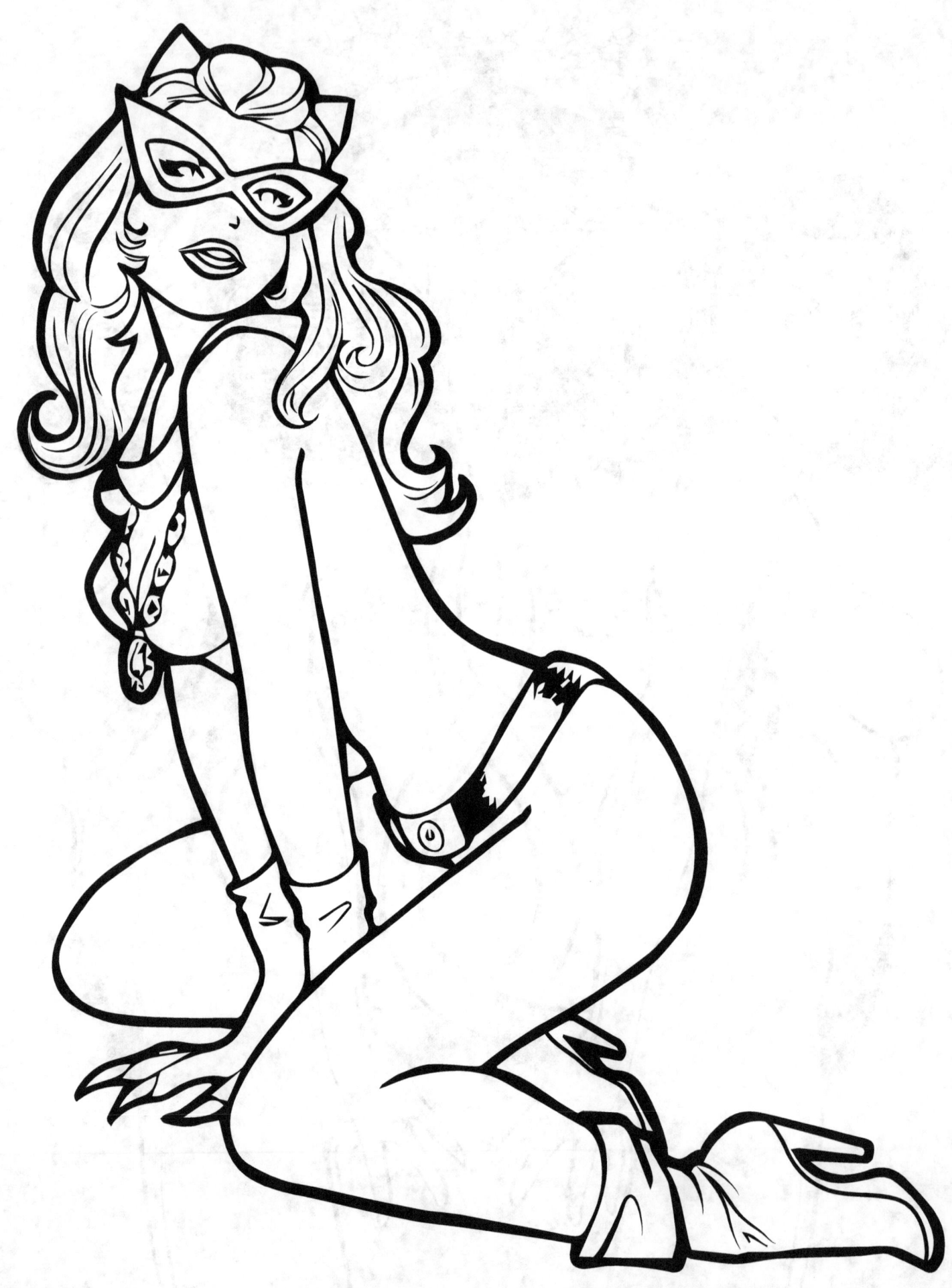

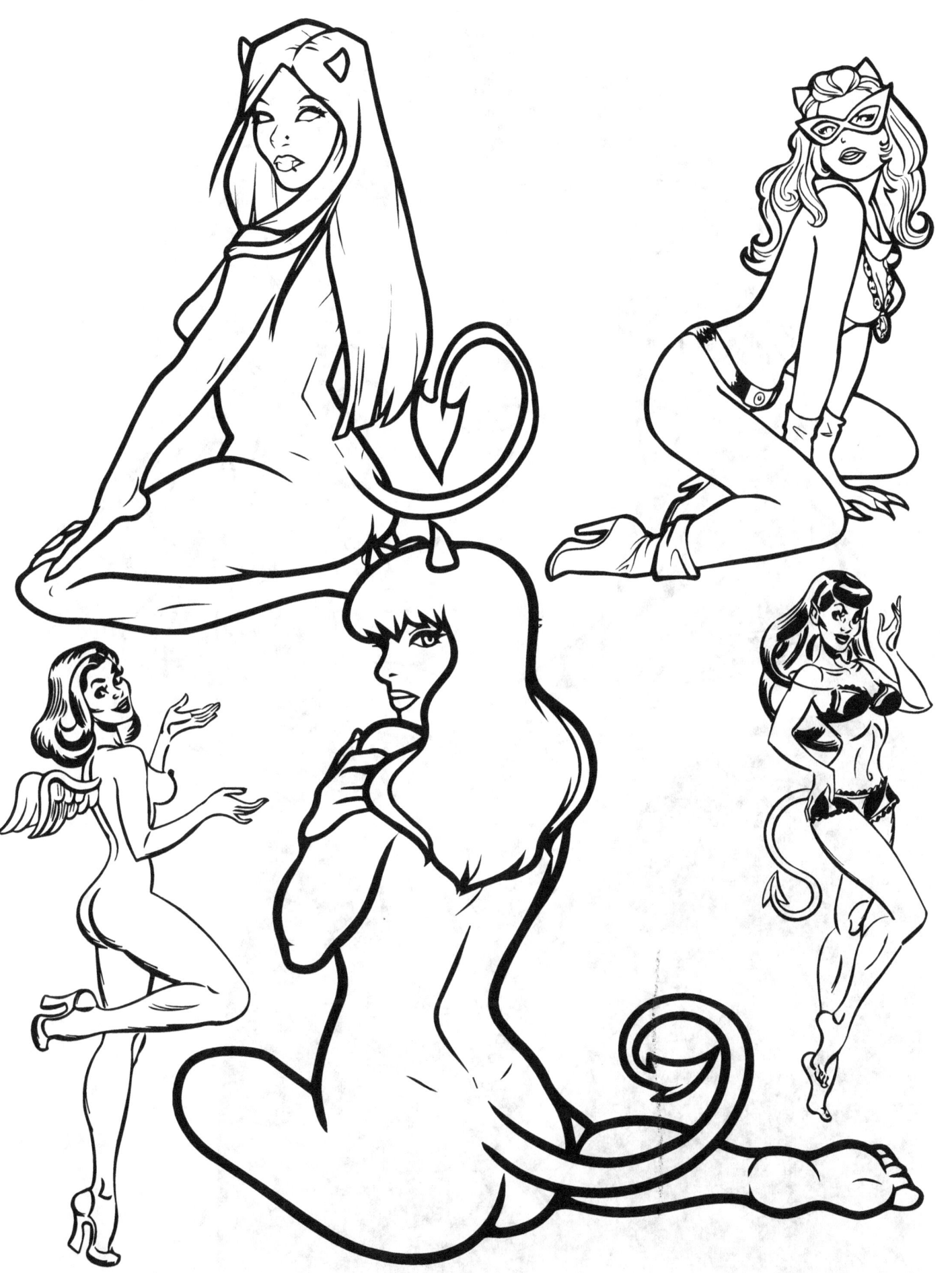

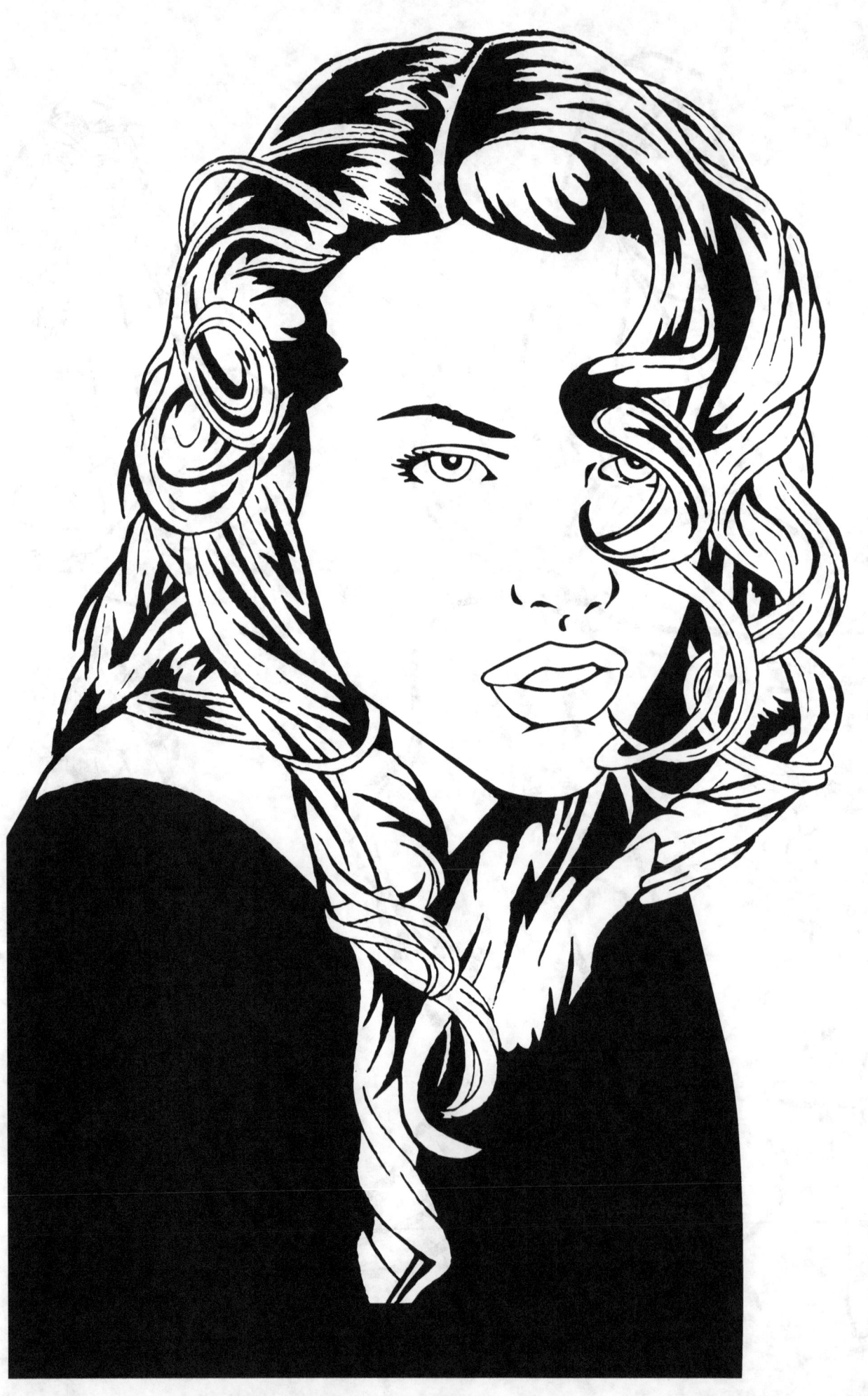

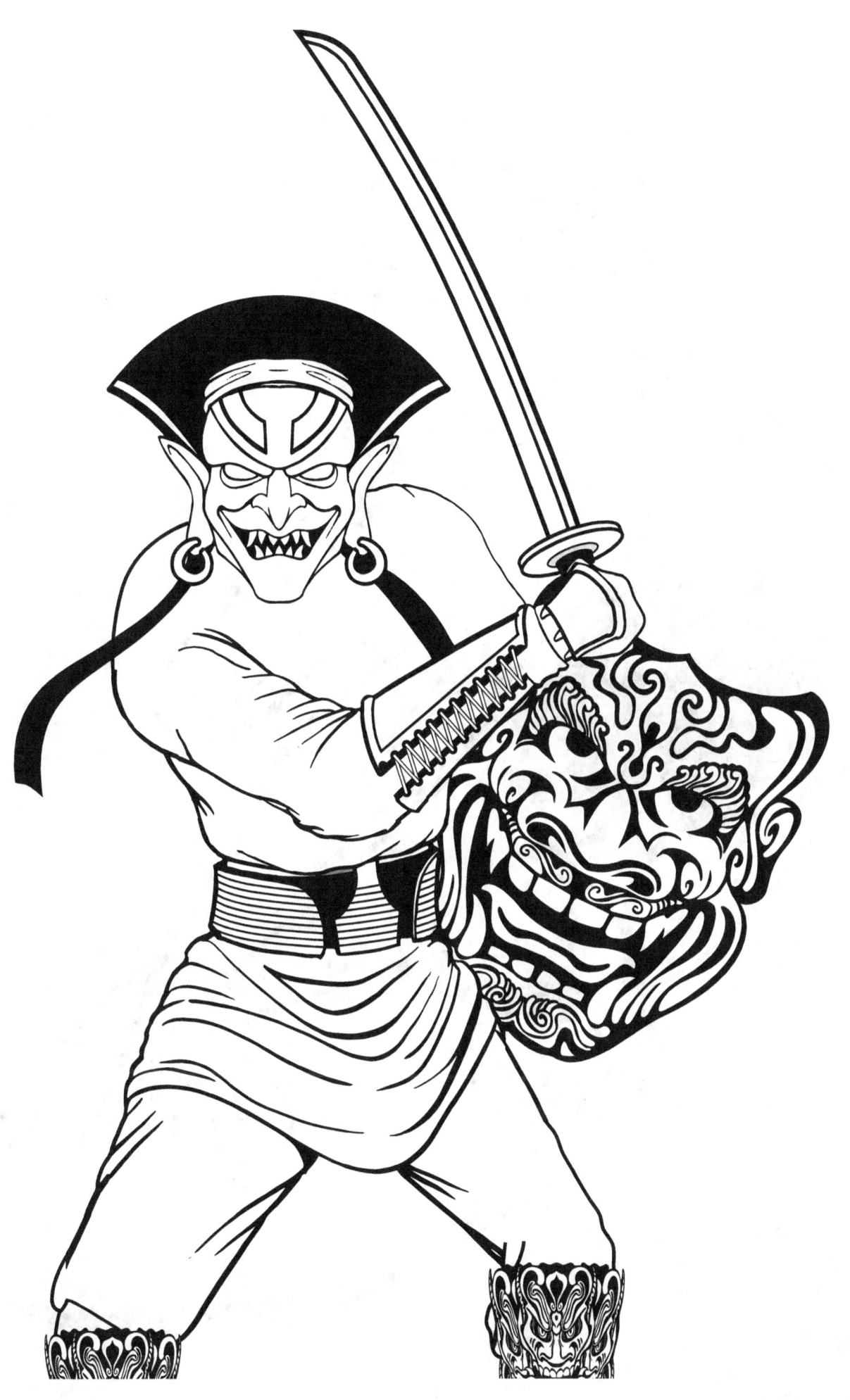

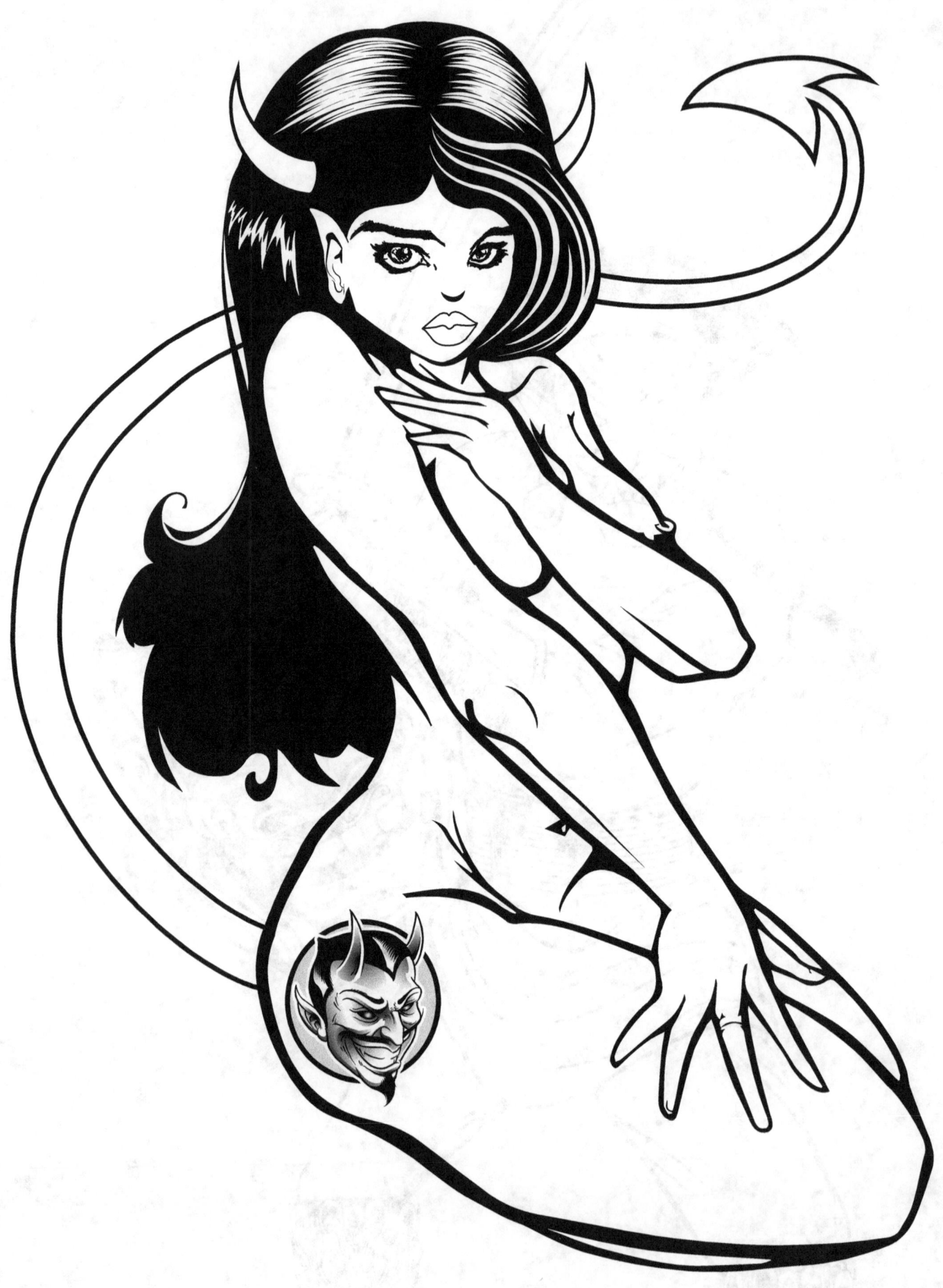

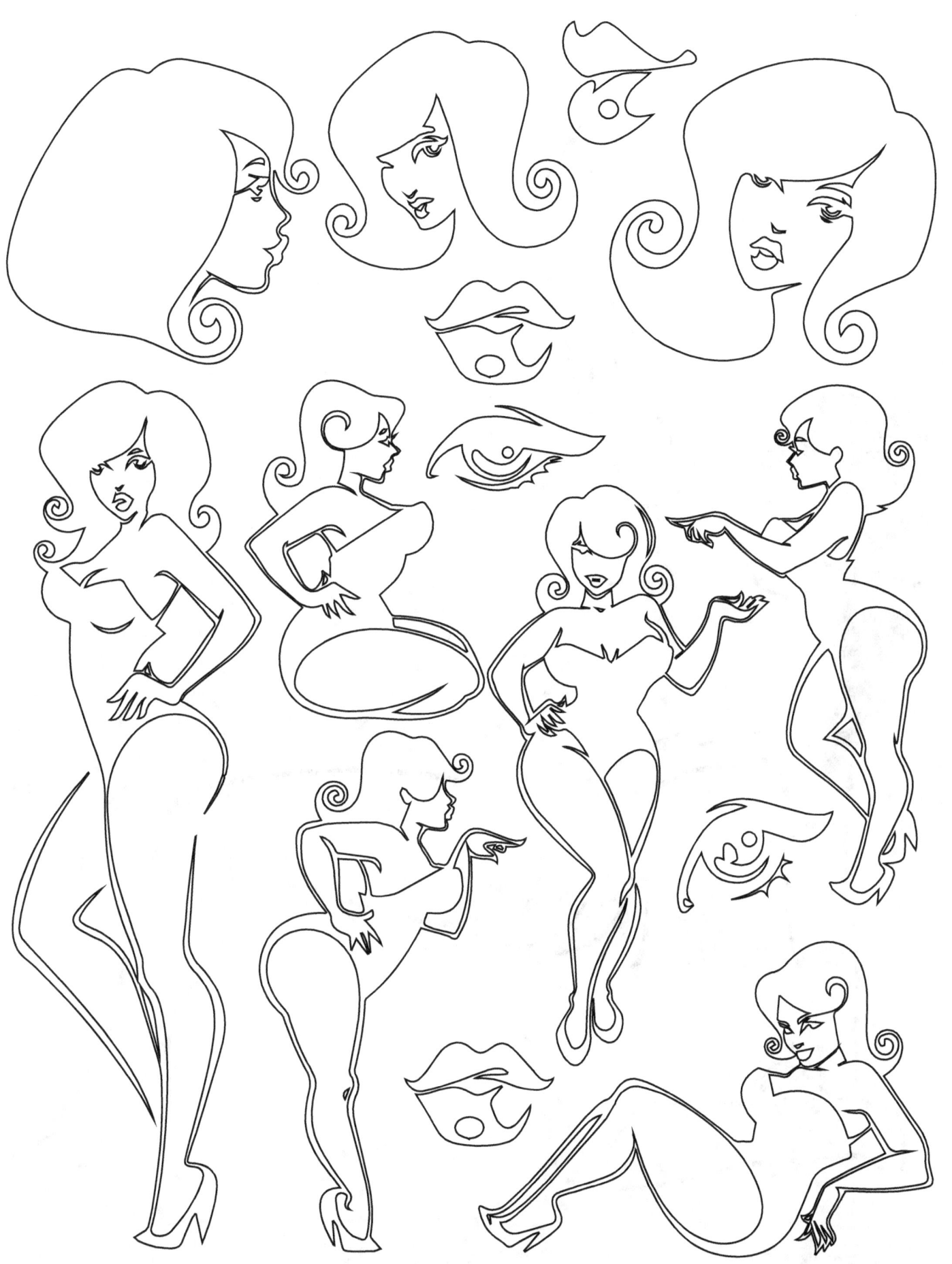

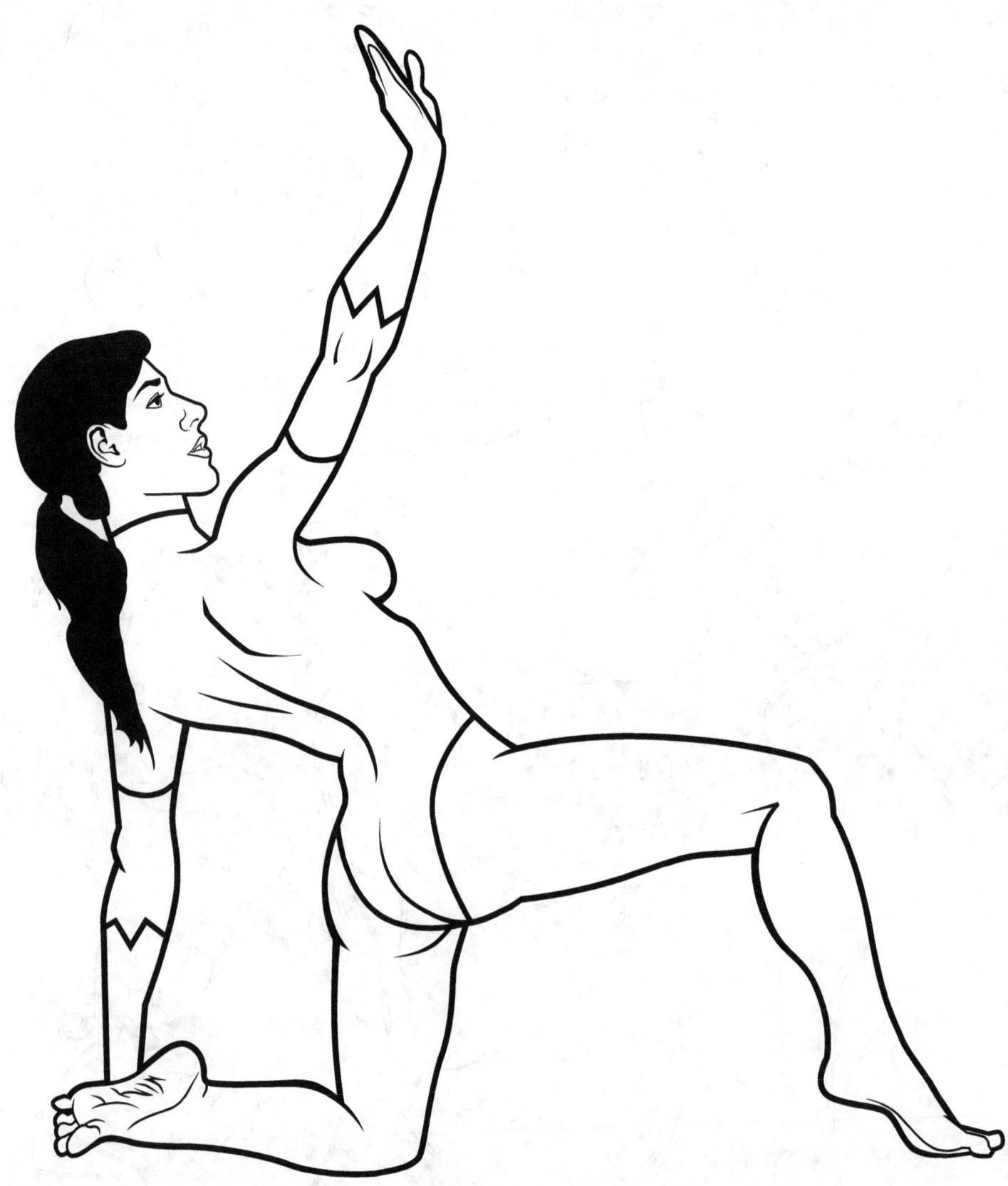

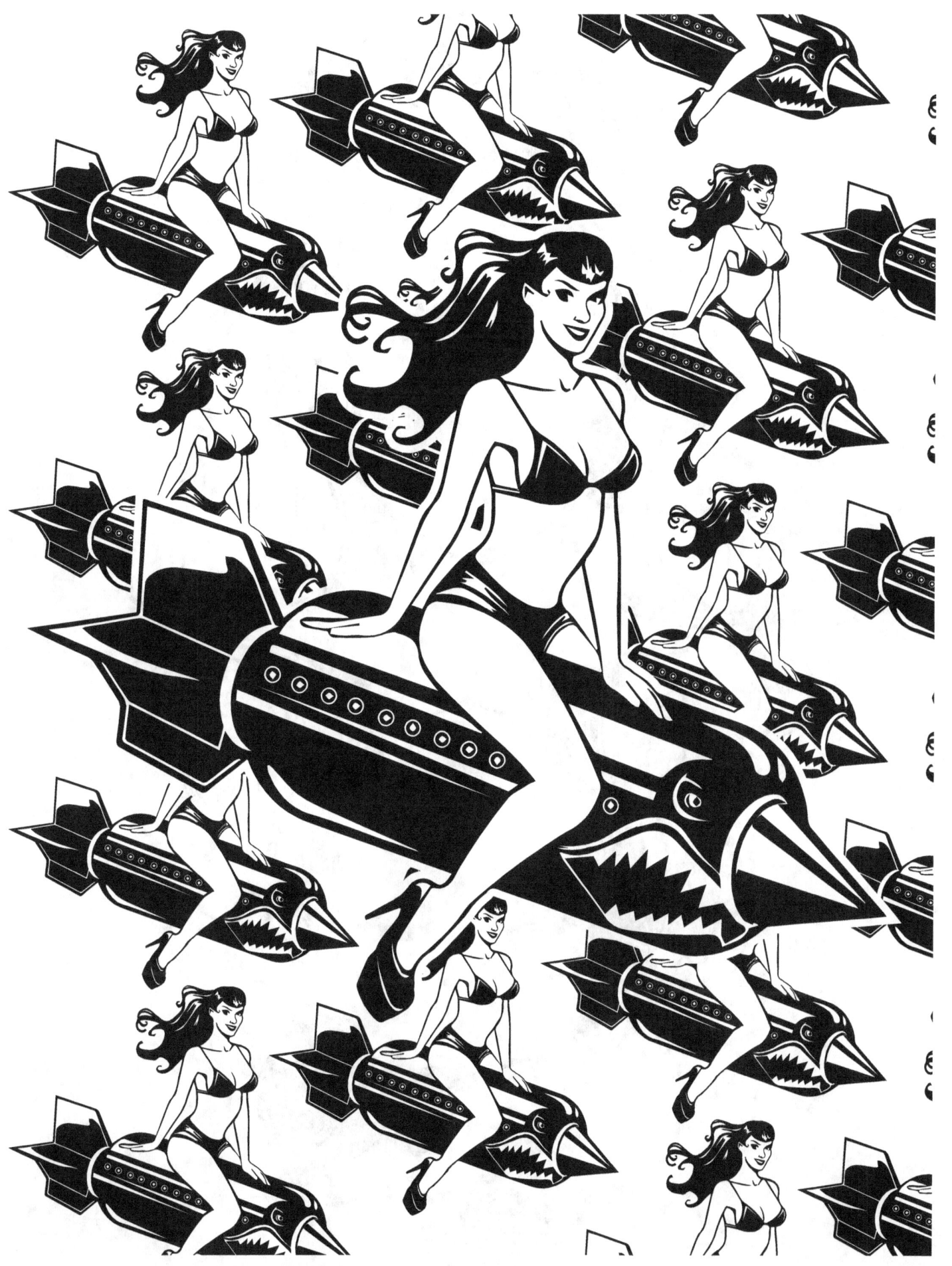

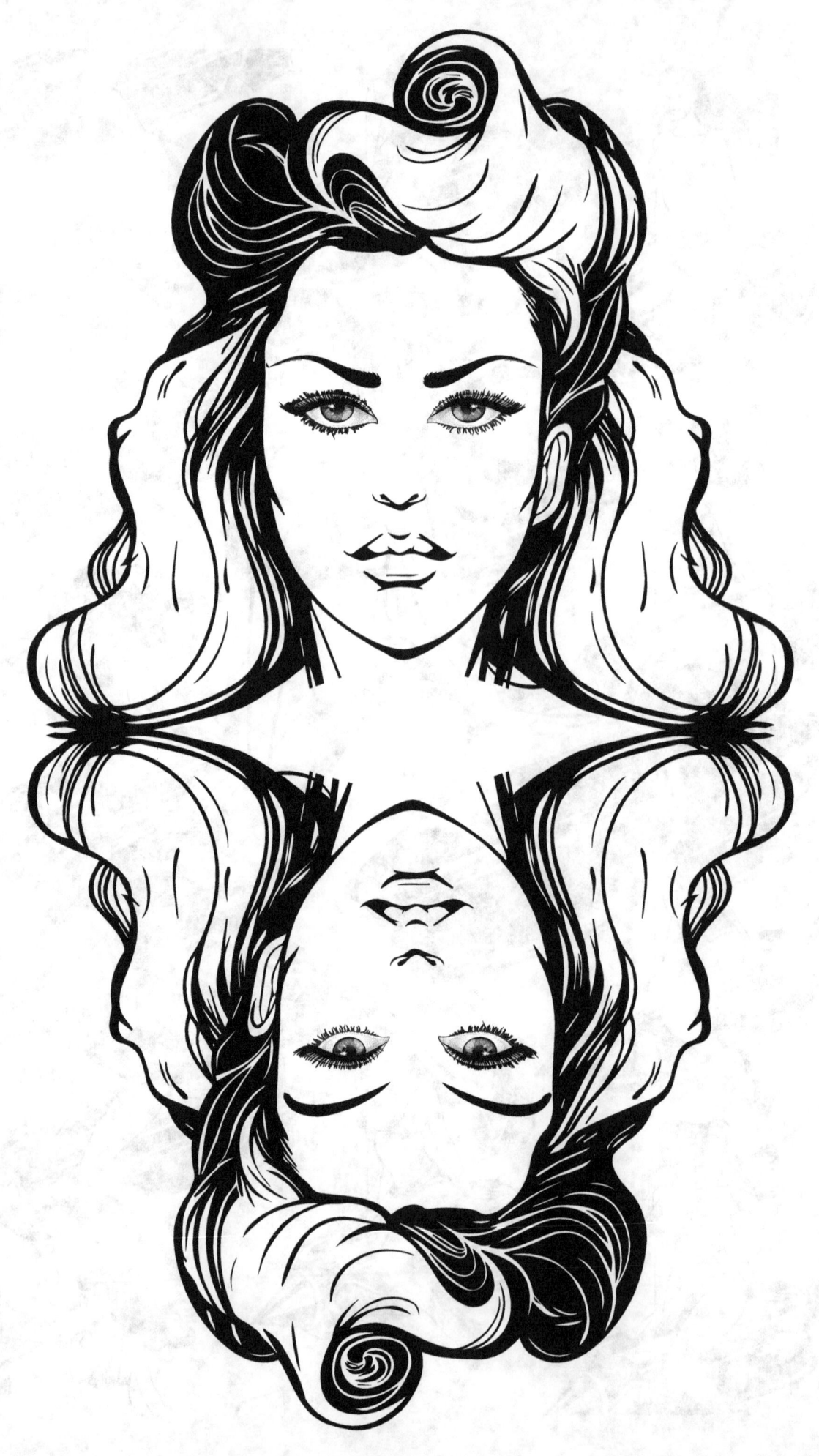

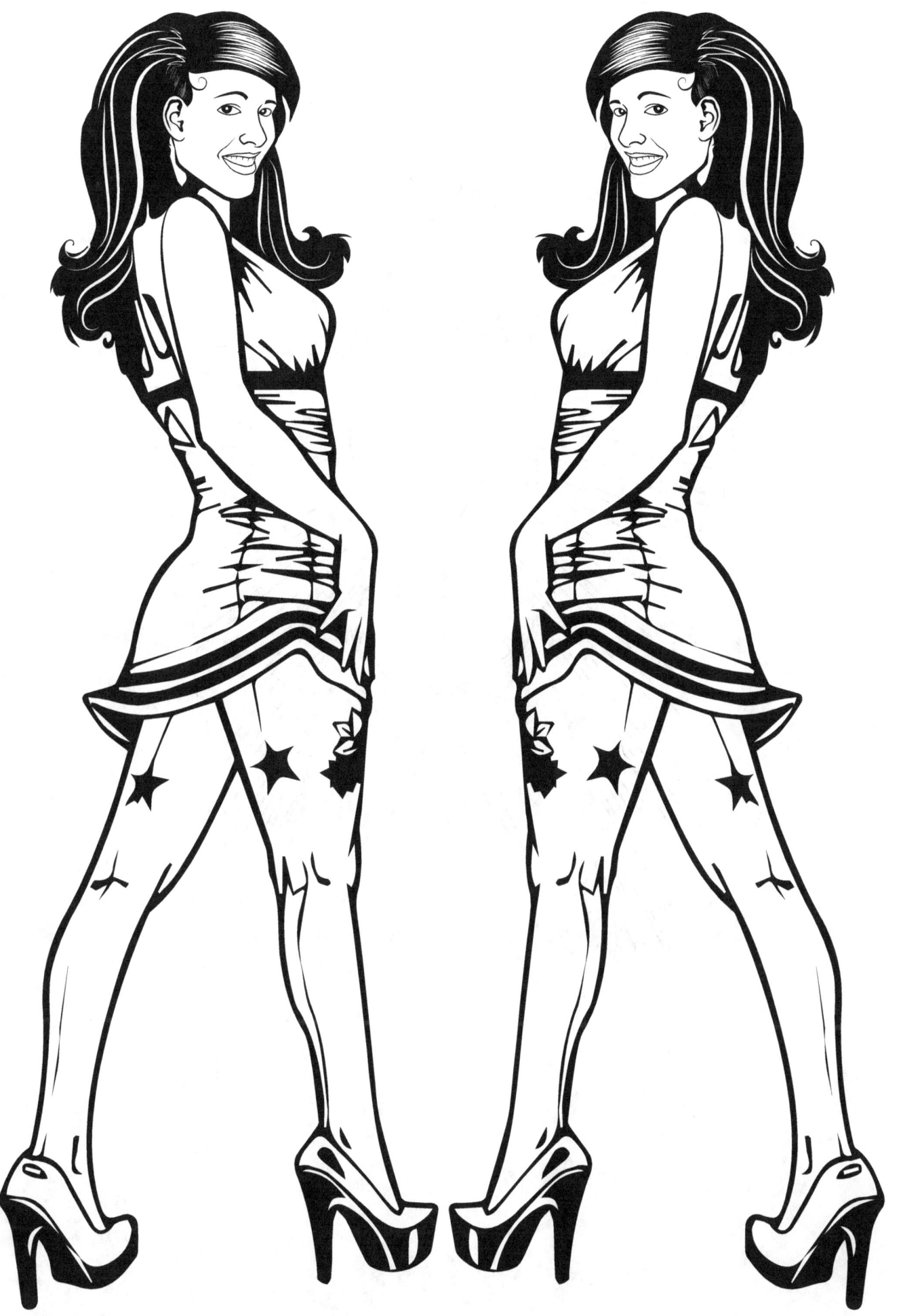

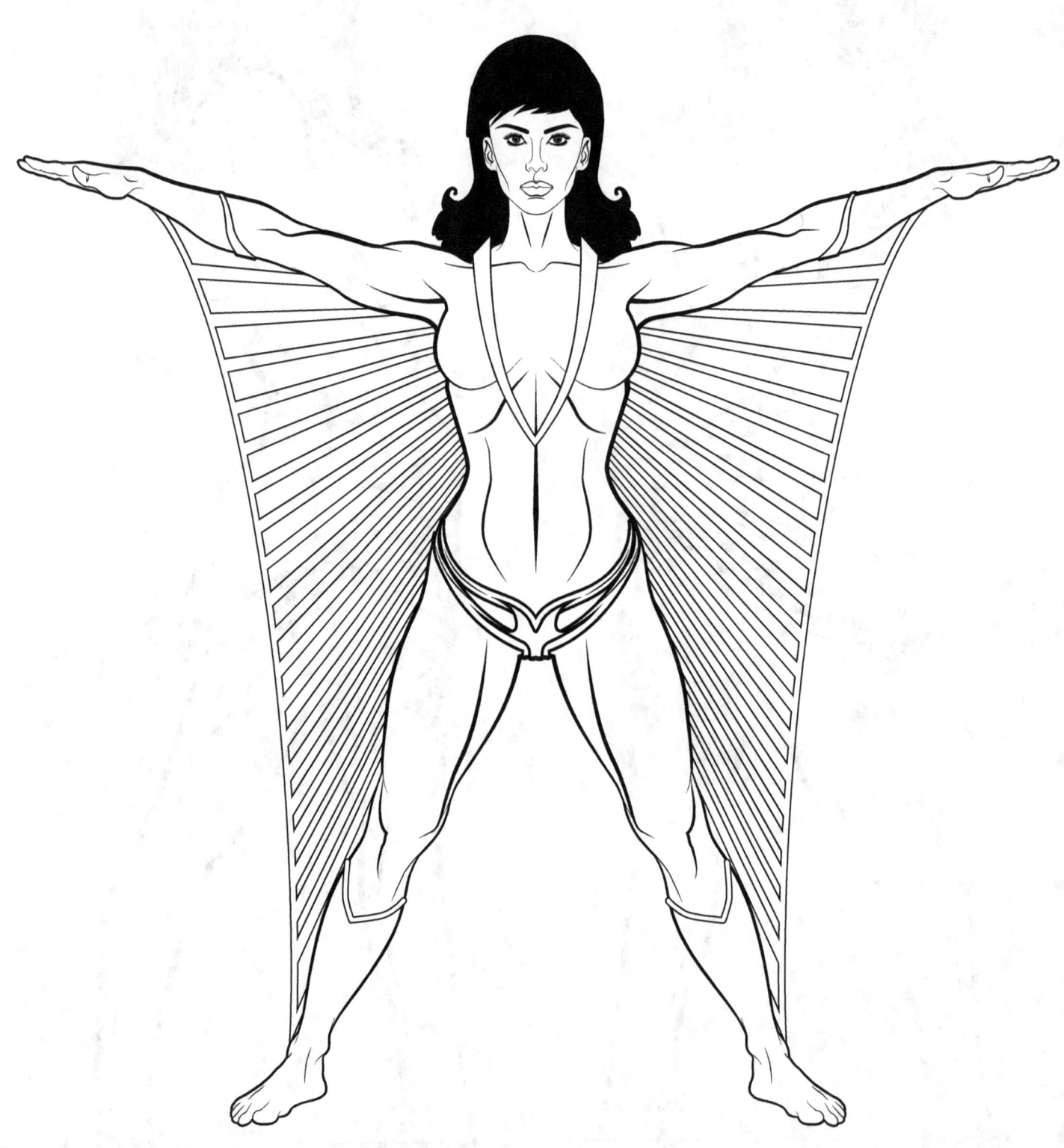

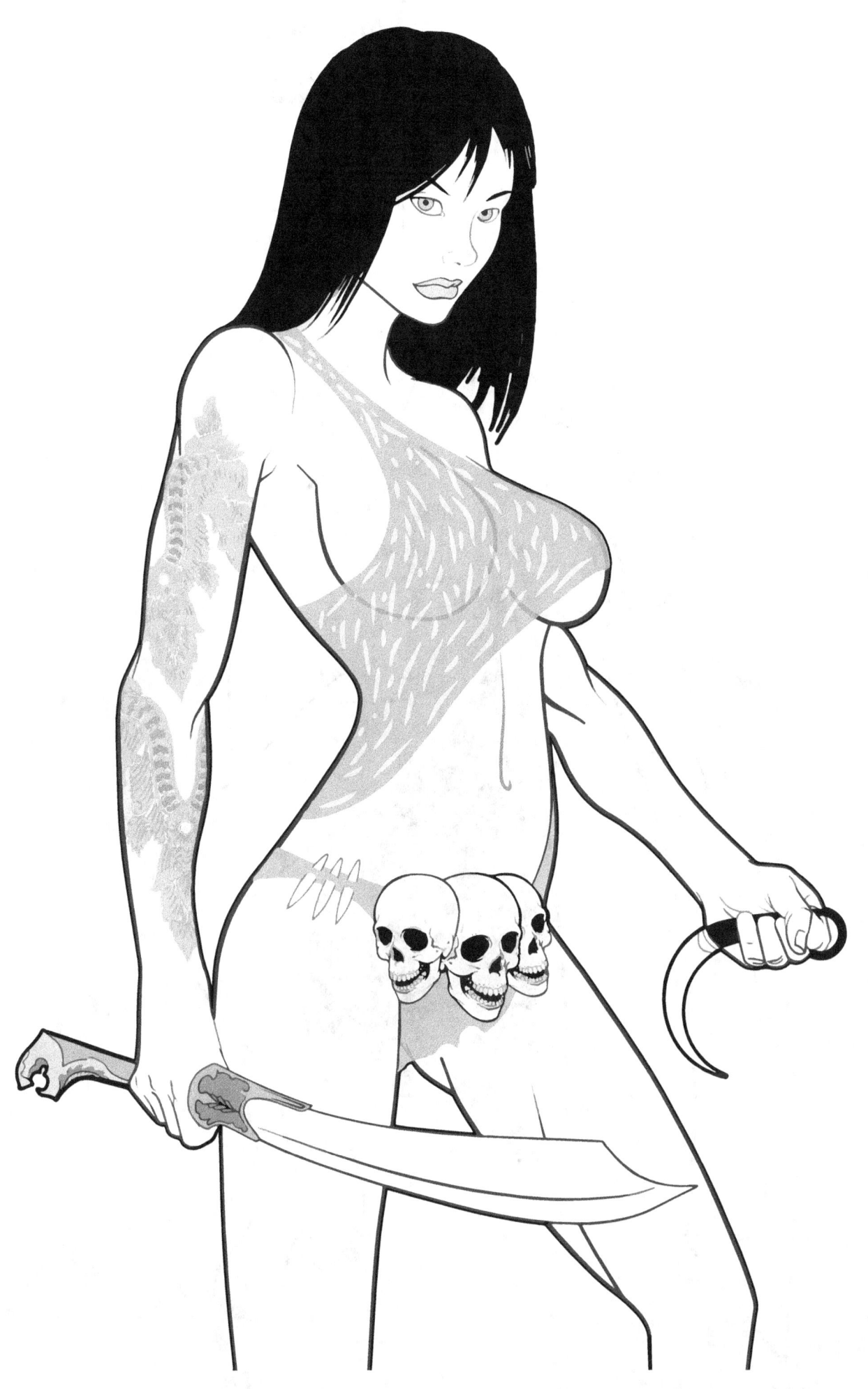

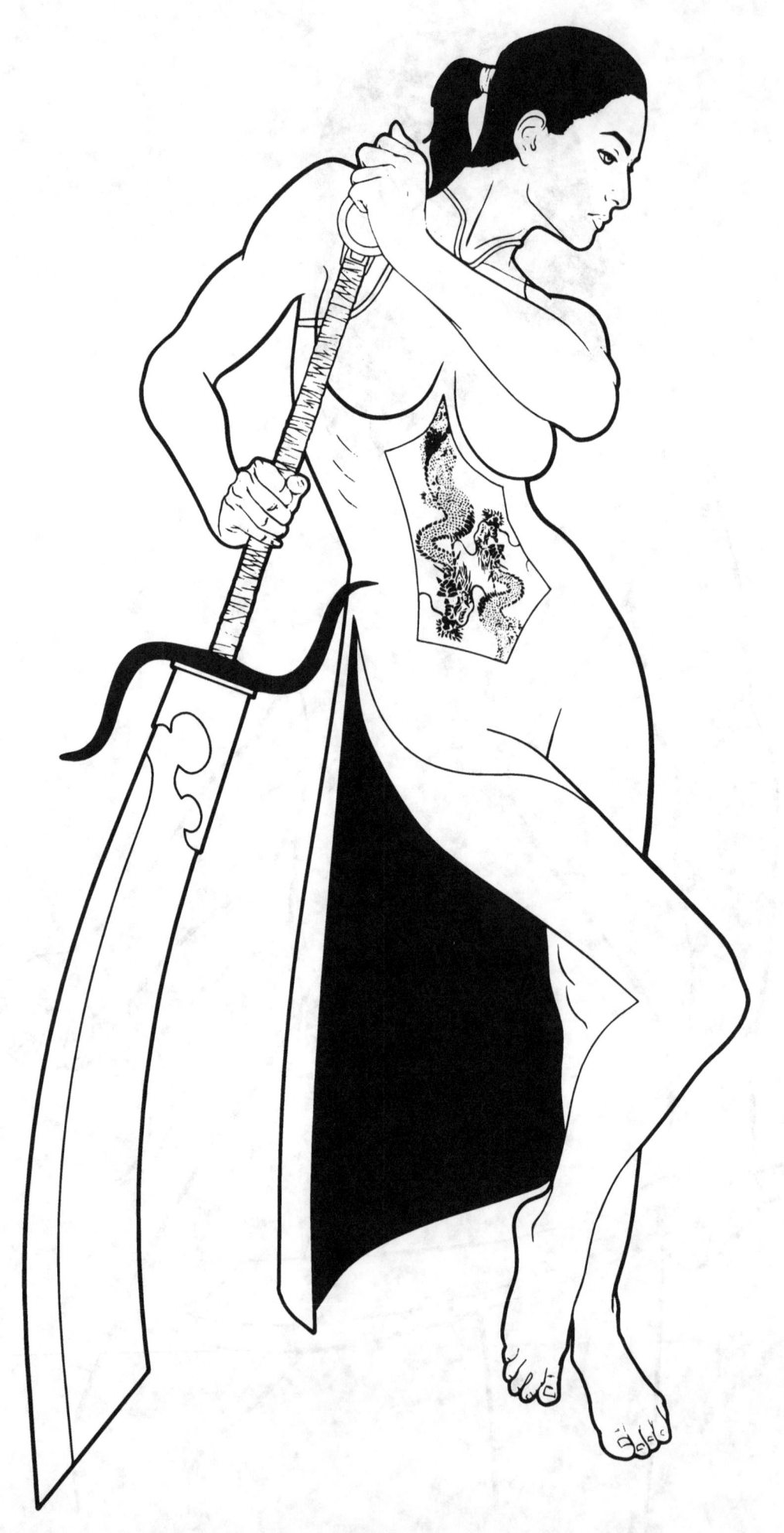

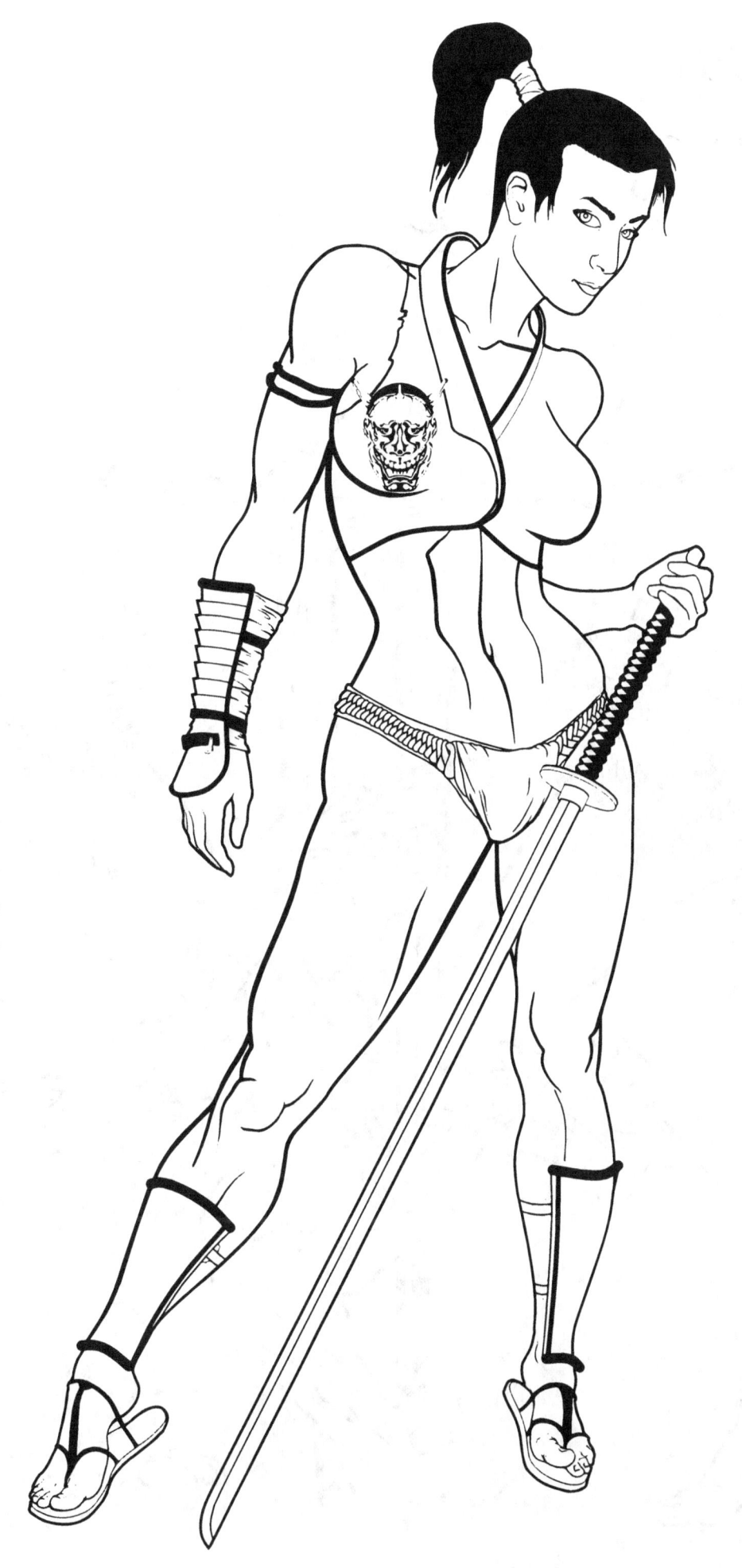

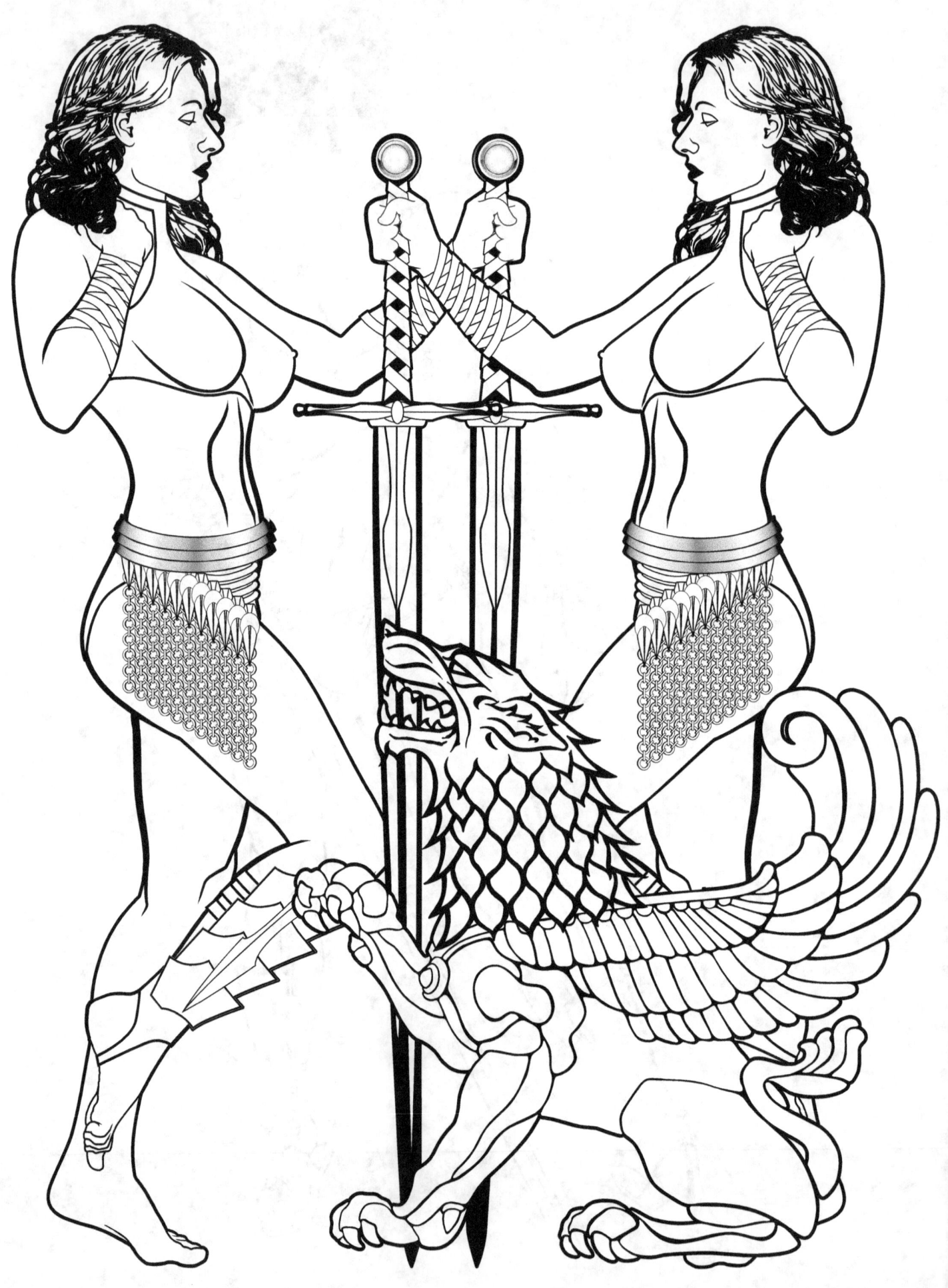

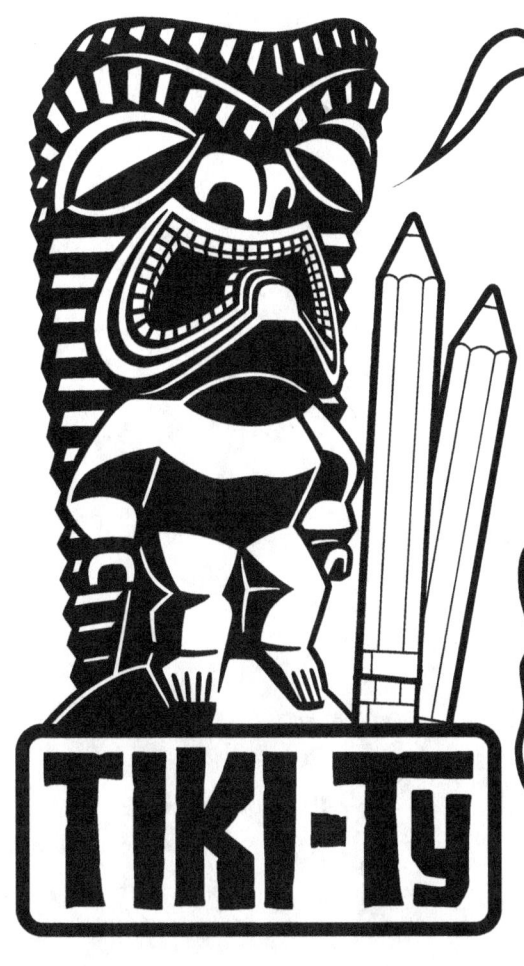

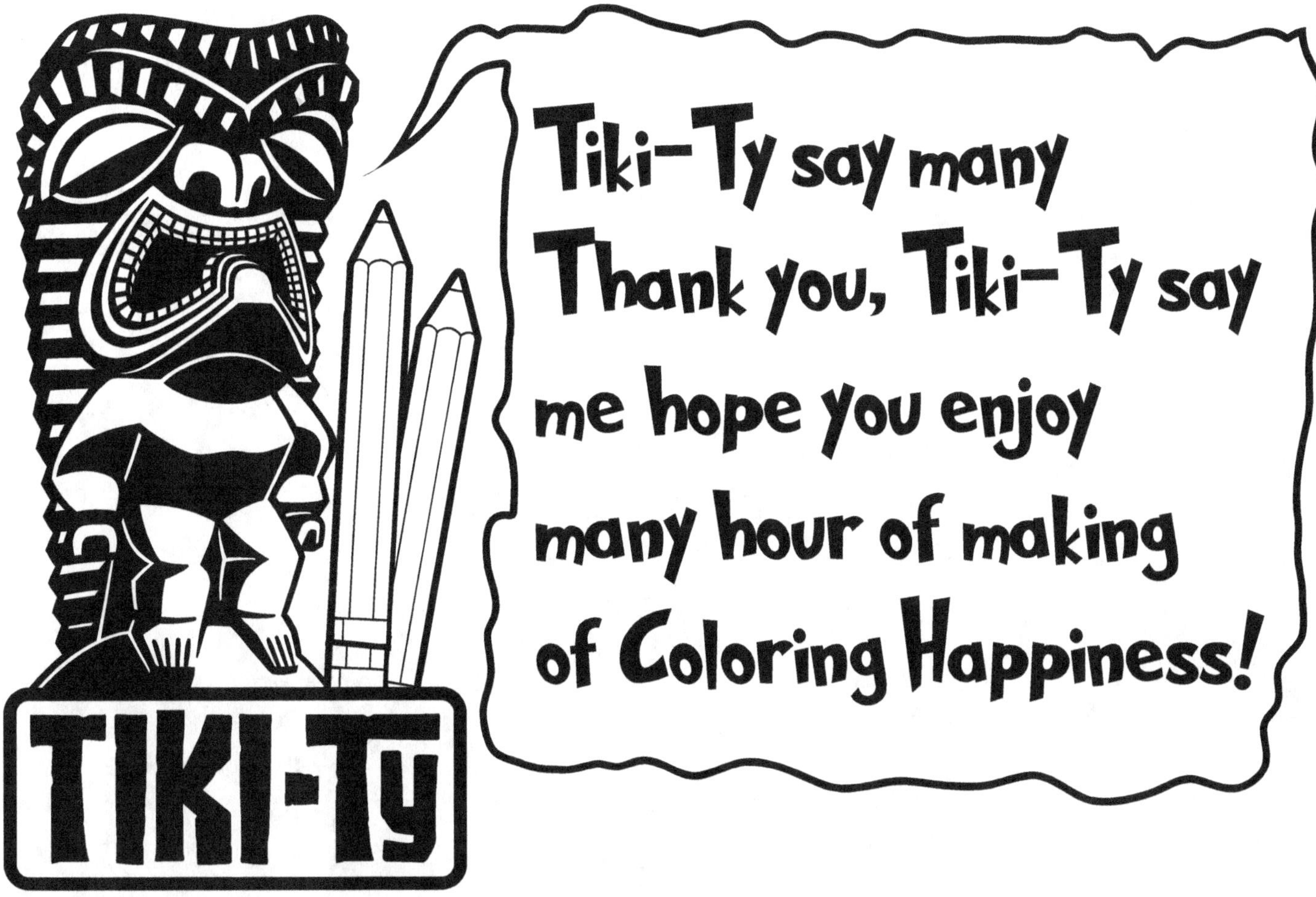

Tiki-Ty say many Thank you, Tiki-Ty say me hope you enjoy many hour of making of Coloring Happiness!

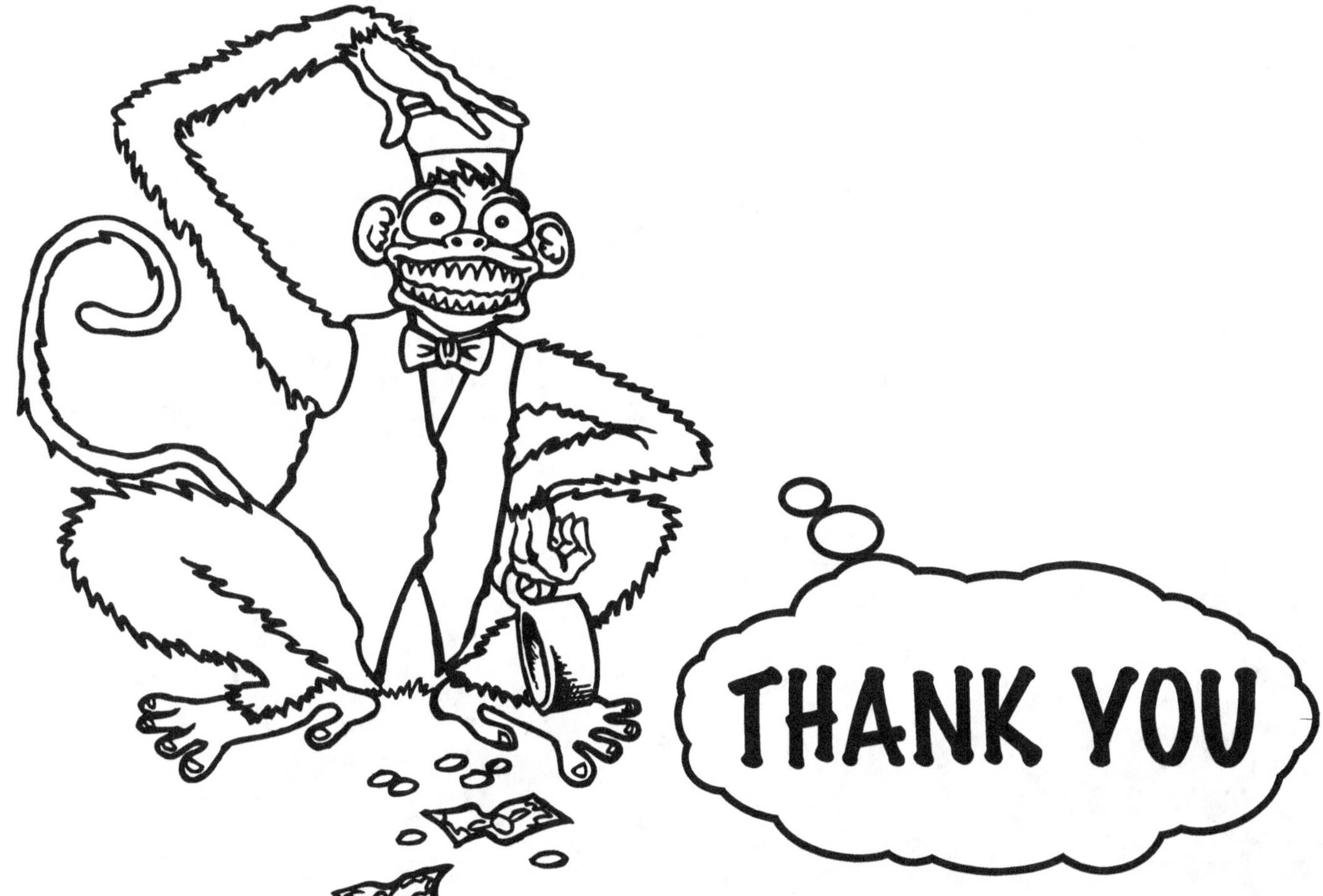

THANK YOU